CASTLES
OF
SHROPSHIRE

CASTLE SITES IN SHROPSHIRE

x Earthwork or Motte and Bailey
▢ Stone Castle
⊠ Earthwork and later stone castle.

CASTLES

OF

SHROPSHIRE

PETER AND ANNE DUCKERS

The History Press

Shropshire is replenished with castles standing thicke on every side

by reason of it was a frontier Country in regard of repelling the Welshmen

in the Marches bordering thereon.

(William Camden: *Britannia* 1607)

First published in 2006 by Tempus Publishing

Reprinted in 2009 by
The History Press
The Mill, Brimscombe Port,
Stroud, Gloucestershire, GL5 2QG
www.thehistorypress.co.uk

British Library Cataloguing in Publication Data.
A catalogue record for this book is available from the British Library.

ISBN 978 0 7524 3645 6

Typesetting and origination by
Tempus Publishing Limited
Printed in Great Britain

CONTENTS

ACKNOWLEDGEMENTS

The authors would like to thank the current editors of the *Victoria County History* for permission to use and adapt sketch maps of various Shropshire sites (identified as VCH/1) taken from Volume I (1908) of the Shropshire edition. They also extend their sincere thanks to the Clwyd-Powys Archaeological Trust (CPAT) in Welshpool for permission to reproduce the aerial photographs included in the text.

It should be noted that most of the sites listed in this work are on private property and permission to visit should always be sought from the local landowner. The authors, who were never denied access to any site and were always met with courtesy and co-operation, wish to thank all those owners who gave permission for them to examine the sites on their land.

INTRODUCTION

England's largest inland county, Shropshire possesses fortifications of all eras, many long pre-dating the introduction of castles *per se*. These include fine examples of prehistoric earthworks, like hill-forts such as Old Oswestry, a Roman town at Wroxeter, a large number of Roman fort sites and important Anglo-Saxon earthworks in the form of the border boundaries of Offa's Dyke and Wat's Dyke. All of these pre-date the familiar medieval castles, nearly 140 of which are scattered around the county. The majority lie to the west, along the Welsh border, with comparatively few in the central and eastern areas.

Castles are usually taken to be defensive structures or defended residences developed in northern France. First introduced into England with the spread of Norman influence in the mid-eleventh century, they were established throughout the country after the Norman invasion of 1066. Indeed, one medieval chronicler born near Shrewsbury, Orderic Vitalis, regarded the construction of castles as the key feature in explaining Norman success in their attempts to control the country.

Shropshire has the largest concentration in England of the castle type known as the motte and bailey, with over 70 examples, and many more lie across the modern border with Wales. The *motte* was an earth mound, man-made or shaped from a natural feature, on which stood timber structures. These could vary from small watchtowers (as at Hockleton) to multi-storeyed buildings, like the wooden *donjon* (keep) which stood until *c.*1270 at Shrewsbury. A large tower would serve as a citadel in time of attack but might contain domestic rooms – residential apartments, storerooms etc. The summit of the motte might be encircled with a wooden palisade and its base by a ditch and bank. The *bailey* was an enclosure lying at the foot of the mound, usually surrounded by its own bank and ditch and defended by a wooden palisade, in which the domestic buildings of the castle were located – barns, stables, houses and even a church on some sites. It is noticeable that many Shropshire mottes stand in close proximity to a church. Since the presence of a stone church with tower would have compromised the castle's security, they presumably lay within the perimeters of the castle (as at Holdgate, Knockin, Little Ness and Ruyton) or were constructed after the castle had ceased to have any military significance.

Of course, not all Norman castles were of the motte and bailey type and there are examples of another form in Shropshire, known as the ringwork. This was a low, flat-topped mound whose internal structures were surrounded by a high earth bank and/or a palisade, with defended gateways and outer ditches. These may pre-date motte and bailey types, representing less developed forms of castle or defended settlement, a theory reinforced by the fact that some Shropshire mottes are known to have been formed from ringworks (e.g. More, Bryn Amlwg, Pontesbury).

The reason for the wealth of early castles in Shropshire is not hard to find. At the time of William I, Shropshire lay on the turbulent Welsh border, an active frontier zone where raids and incursions were common – and had been for generations. The consolidation of Norman power in the region known as the Welsh Marches was a major priority between 1070-1100. Shropshire was divided into nine sizeable lordships where leading Norman lords were given extensive powers in return for imposing Norman rule and stabilising the area. Strategic considerations apart, this was an area where new foreign landowners might look to their security amongst a people not likely to welcome their presence and their castles were not only defended residences but intimidating symbols of power and superiority.

The largest block of estates in Shropshire was granted to the king's kinsman Roger 'of Montgomery' (1022-94). One of William's most trusted supporters, Roger was left in control of William's Norman territories during the invasion and came to England in 1067, to be created Earl of Arundel later that year. He was granted estates in nine counties, notably Sussex and Shropshire and around 1071 was created Earl of Shrewsbury. From the new castle there Roger advanced into Wales where he founded, *c.*1074, the original castle of Montgomery, named after the family homeland of Ste. Foy de Montgomery in Calvados. Earl Roger's main tenants established a network of castles along the Welsh border and along major valley routes, many located as one would expect in areas offering strategic advantage – guarding road routes, crossroads and river crossings, controlling river valleys, or on heights dominating the landscape. The cluster of mottes along the Rea Brook and Camlad valleys – a major route into Wales – is a good example.

Early castles could vary greatly in their function and size. Some were important garrisons or administrative centres – as with Shrewsbury and Ludlow, both important bases on the Welsh frontier. Some Shropshire castles, like Ludlow, Caus, Clun, More and Bishop's Castle, became centres of new planned towns, the castle-with-borough being the principal Norman contribution to the urbanisation of England. Many of Shropshire's early castles are, however, very small – little more than defended farmsteads – and some, especially those sited near surviving farms, deserted hamlets or in places of little military significance, may relate to a deliberate attempt to settle the western areas of the county after 1100.

Whatever their origins, the remains of most of these early castles are far from impressive. Many are little more than tree-covered mounds in a field, with all traces of ditches, baileys and domestic buildings long decayed or ploughed away. But we should not be deceived by their present appearance; in their day, some represented state-of-the-art military engineering. Nor should we consider that these castles, despite their catch-all designation as 'motte and bailey' types, were necessarily standardised in shape, construction or scale. There were undoubtedly variations in the way that timber defences and buildings were constructed and in the size and nature of the buildings within the castle's perimeters. Over time, reflecting changes in the power and wealth of the landowner or the security of the area, defensive perimeters could be extended or reduced and might be adapted or abandoned. In sites which *were* abandoned or destroyed, only archaeological excavation can reveal the nature of the castle and give some indication of the lifestyle of its inhabitants. Unfortunately, less than a third of Shropshire's castles have any surviving documentary references and few have received any archaeological investigation, so that much about them remains conjectural.

Earth and timber castles were relatively easy to build and maintain and answered the need of a new warrior aristocracy in a turbulent area where speed of construction was a priority. However, given increased wealth, relative stability and time, stronger defences could be constructed. In a few cases – Ludlow being the prime Shropshire example – castles were built in stone from the beginning. But most of the castles which survived much into the twelfth century began to replace their earth and timber defences with stone, as at Shrewsbury, Hodnet, Little Shrawardine and elsewhere. The experience of England's warrior aristocracy during the early phases of the Crusades is one often-cited reason for the development of stone castles. Whatever its cause, in the twelfth century the use of stone began to be reflected in Shropshire. Stone *donjons* (or keeps), curtain walls and elaborate gateway defences replaced simpler earth and timber structures. In some cases, redevelopment must have been a slow process and timber may have remained in use as a primary building material for longer than is often thought. It is worth recalling that Shrewsbury – a royal castle and administrative centre – retained its wooden *donjon* as late as *c.*1270, when it collapsed into the Severn. This was long after the construction of stone walls, towers and gateways in the castle itself and the appearance of stone walls around the town of Shrewsbury.

As the Welsh border stabilised after *c.*1300 following Edward I's campaigns, the military significance of many of Shropshire's westernmost castles declined. Although the owners of less defensive residences, like Acton Burnell or Cheney Longville, applied for licence to crenellate – official permission to add battlements and strengthen walls – this was generally to increase local status rather than a serious attempt to fortify a residence. The many moated sites in Shropshire, indicating the simpler defences of a house or farm, may reflect the process of moving towards more practical domestic structures, often built near the site of the old castle (e.g. Aston Botterell, Willaston, Cressage). The number of Shropshire castle sites immediately next to a church or close to an old-established farm may be other indications of the decline of the military function of the castle and the continuation of a purely domestic or farming settlement nearby.

Some castles remained in use because of their local or even national significance – Ludlow (the seat of the Council of Wales) being one example. However, even status as a royal castle did not guarantee survival, since most were victims of the regular lack of royal funds; a report on Shrewsbury Castle in 1443, for example, makes it clear that it was near collapse.

The majority of Shropshire's castles were deserted or in various degrees of dilapidation by the early sixteenth century. An insight into their state at that time is given by the *Itinerary*, compiled between 1539-45 by Henry VIII's antiquarian, John Leland (1506-52), who records little but ruin in most cases. The last employment of Shropshire's castles in a military sense came during the Civil Wars of 1642-51 when there was a flurry of activity to refortify castles which in many cases had been ruinous for generations. Many were damaged in the fighting which followed, either as a direct result of military operations or by deliberate slighting to render them militarily useless, as at Hopton, Bridgnorth, Lea, Shrawardine, Oswestry and others.

A few castles remain because they were incorporated into other buildings or into working farms. Moreton Corbet, for example, became part of a sixteenth-century Renaissance mansion (never completed), and Lea, Wattlesborough, Cheney Longville and Holdgate were integrated into working farms. Some found inglorious use as windmill bases or gazebo mounds or as 'romantic' ruins in planned landscapes (as at Redcastle). Most gradually vanished as their military value or residential desirability declined and their materials were removed for re-use elsewhere. Many of the larger rural castles like Corfham, Charlton and Caus and many of the urban examples, like Wem, Bridgnorth, Whitchurch, Oswestry, Ellesmere and Pontesbury, were simply left to decay and over time were robbed of their materials so that they were gradually reduced or removed altogether.

Today, few of the castles of Shropshire remain useable in any practical sense. Some do so after much alteration – neither Rowton nor Sibdon Carwood have anything of their medieval structure remaining, Shrewsbury houses a museum and Broncroft is a country house. For the rest, we are left to tramp muddy fields looking for grassy, tree-capped mounds, overgrown banks, shallow ditches or isolated fragments of masonry to remind us of the wealth of castle building which once existed in Shropshire.

The scope of the gazetteer

The further one goes back in time, the less relevance the modern Shropshire border has to the location and study of the region's castles. In historical terms, the motte and bailey castles in western Shropshire should be considered alongside (for example) the 50 or so lying across the border in Montgomeryshire. The whole group should be regarded as one historical entity associated with the consolidation of Norman power on the Welsh frontier. However, since the present book is intended as a *county* guide, the authors have, with the exception of Bishop's Moat (q.v.), stuck to its present boundaries, however interesting other nearby examples might be.

The authors have visited every castle listed in this book where anything significant remains above ground. The photographs, with the exception of the aerial views, were taken in 2005, mainly in the autumn and winter months when there was less foliage to obscure the sites.

Main Map references are to the Ordnance Survey's current 'Landranger' 1:50,000 series. A star rating system has been introduced to help identify the more interesting sites:

★ = worth visiting as an interesting example of its type.
★★ = a very good example of its type or of special interest.
★★★ = an outstanding site.

(The sites with no star rating are considered to be less significant than the others.)

THE GAZETTEER

Acton Bank SO 315850

The faint traces of an earthwork on Acton Bank Hill were regarded as nothing more than an eroded burial mound until aerial photography suggested an alternative interpretation. The remains appear to be those of a motte with associated baileys. The mound, lying on a south-west facing slope overlooking the route between Bishop's Castle and Clun, was about 27m in diameter, though now almost entirely ploughed away. Aerial photography also revealed a bailey lying to the south of the motte and another enclosure to its south-west. Nothing is known of its origins or history.

Acton Burnell SJ 534019 ★★★

Actune was one of 25 manors held by Roger Fitz Corbet in 1086 and become part of the Corbet Barony of Caus; the Burnell family were tenants by the late twelfth century. Bishop Robert Burnell built the 'castle' at Acton Burnell between 1283-6. Appointed Lord Chancellor in 1274 and Bishop of Bath and Wells in 1275, Burnell was an important political figure under Edward I and also built the Bishop's Palace at Wells, with which Acton Burnell has some stylistic affinities. The Bishop entertained Edward I at Acton Burnell in 1282 and 1283, probably in a manor house which pre-dated the surviving

1 The outline of a probable motte and bailey at Acton Bank, revealed by aerial photography. *CPAT-86-MB-1029*

castle (see below). The bishop, who held other Shropshire manors including Cound and the Barony of Holdgate, was responsible for extending the village of Acton Burnell and for rebuilding the church of St Mary to the north-west of the castle.

After Bishop Burnell's death at Berwick in 1292 the house remained in family possession until *c.*1428. In 1452 it passed to William, Lord Lovell, and from him descended through various other families. Perhaps abandoned as early as 1420, it may have been reoccupied by the Crompton family in the mid-sixteenth century. It appears to have played no part in the Civil War but

2 The north and west sides of Acton Burnell, viewed from the adjacent churchyard. The roof of the central block is eighteenth century or later

3 The south wall of Acton Burnell with the large gateway cut through in the eighteenth century

was inhabited by the Smythe family as late as 1660 (before the construction of their new mansion to the north) and was finally abandoned by 1672. Thereafter, its ruins were used as farm buildings.

The surviving castle of red and grey sandstone is a three-storey oblong, internally 21 x 15.5m, around what is now an open court, with four-storey towers at each corner and a small block between the towers on the west side. Apart from adaptations for farm use in the eighteenth century, it shows no sign of significant alteration over generations and can be regarded as the product of one building phase in the late thirteenth century.

The ground floor housed a buttery and other domestic rooms. The first floor was occupied on its eastern side by a large, rectangular Great Hall lit with tall, two-light windows, three in the north wall and three in the south. The western side of this storey contained the Great Chamber, or audience room, above which were the bishop's private apartments, the whole corresponding to the height of the adjoining hall (*colour plate 14*).

The small west block had storerooms on the ground floor, a garderobe on the upper floor and above that a small chamber. Its roof is modern. The four projecting corner towers were little more than staircase and latrine blocks. The north-west tower (part of which collapsed in 1914) housed a storeroom and garderobe, whilst those on the south-west and south-east carried staircases. The north-east tower, partially demolished in the eighteenth century, was larger, with a chapel on the first floor as well as a staircase. At roof level, a wall-walk connected the uppermost rooms in the towers. There were battlemented parapets, well preserved on the north-west tower, Bishop Burnell having been granted licence to crenellate in 1284. Nevertheless, the castle's defensive capabilities were poor – its walls average only 1m thick and are pierced by a number of large windows and doorways.

However, it should be borne in mind that what now remains is only the kernel of the complex which once occupied the site. The bishop was an important man with a large retinue, befitting his status. In his day there would have been other buildings nearby (probably in timber) to accommodate guests, officials, retainers and visitors seeking audience with the chancellor, as well as functional buildings like stables, a kitchen, barns etc. Some evidence of attached buildings (e.g. service hatches and access doors) can be seen in the east wall of the block. In terms of actual defence, a separate stone gatehouse is recorded in 1548 but there are no traces of moats or defensive earthworks near the castle.

In the eighteenth century, when the ruins were used as a barn, numerous alterations were made. These include the large archways through the north and south walls to allow access by carts and the distinctive stone roofs over the west block and south-west tower.

Standing in the fields 90m east of the castle are the remains of a long building, now represented only by its two stone gable ends, 13m wide and 52m apart. Usually described as a tithe barn, it was known as the Parliament House and is by tradition the site of Edward I's Parliament of 1283, where the Statute of Acton Burnell was enacted. Its ruins may be those of a domestic building or part of an earlier complex pre-dating the present castle. Leland called Acton Burnell 'a goodly manor place and Castel where a Parliament was kept in a greate barne'.

Adderley SJ 665404 ★

At the time of Domesday, Adderley was one of four Shropshire manors held of Earl Roger by Nigel 'the Doctor', physician to William I and possibly to Earl Roger. After Nigel's death in 1095, his holdings passed successively to Earl Roger's sons but following the rebellion of Robert in 1102, all were forfeited to the Crown and were granted by Henry I to the Dunstanville family as one estate. Nigel or one of Earl Roger's sons was presumably responsible for the construction of the imposing mound which stands in the grounds of Pool House off the A529, 600m north-east of Adderley.

4 The motte at Adderley (in trees, left) with Pool House to the right

The large motte, derived from a natural feature, stands near two ponds from which the modern farm takes its name. Once known as 'Ethelred's castle', the motte is very steep-sided, standing to approximately 10m high. The summit is irregularly shaped, the result of subsidence or digging (it was used as a pets' cemetery *c.*1930), and extends to about 35 x 17m. It has a modern brick tunnel and ice-house built into its south-east face. There are traces of a ditch between the mound and the farm, whose buildings may stand on the site of the bailey, though nothing visible remains of it. Excavation and scattered pottery finds showed that the site was occupied till the end of the thirteenth century but it never seems to have carried masonry buildings and nothing is known of its history.

Alberbury SJ 357144 *

The Saxon manor of Alberbury was held by King Edward before the conquest and passed to Earl Roger. It was held of him by a 'Roger', who was presumably Roger Corbet since it became part of the holdings of the Corbets of Caus. The first definitely identifiable Corbet owner was Robert Corbet 'the fat', who gave Alberbury church to Shrewsbury Abbey *c.*1145. The Fitz Warine family (under Fulk Fitz Warine I) later became tenants and it is thought that the castle was constructed by Fulk Fitz Warine II before 1220. The castle, which was the *caput* or centre of the manor, was strategically located on the frontier but lies in a somewhat weak position, on rising land above the flood plain of the Severn, presumably to command the valley route, but overlooked by high ground to its south.

Alberbury castle was destroyed by Llewellyn 'the Great' in 1223 and was rebuilt *c.*1226, with a stone wall around its bailey. It remained in Fitz Warine hands until the mid-fourteenth century when it may have been abandoned or at least lost any military significance. It is interesting that the church tower of St Michael and All Angels, only 70m away, was constructed *c.*1290; since this would have compromised the security of the castle, one might assume that it was militarily redundant by then. In the 1540s Leland refers to 'the ruins of Fulk Guarine, the noble warriors castell' at Alberbury.

The keep may have been intermittently re-used as a residence or as a lodge to Loton Park Hall after its reconstruction in the late seventeenth century but was certainly in ruins by the end of the eighteenth century.

The remaining structure, recently cleared of the ivy which had shrouded it for years, is a two-storey stone keep, built to the south-west of the bailey. Standing to a height of approximately 9m, it is constructed of local Alberbury breccia, its doorways and windows originally faced with dressed sandstone, most of which has been robbed away. The keep measures approximately 17 x 13m, with walls up to 2.5m thick. The ground level was probably a storeroom, with a hall and private chambers on the first floor. The hall's entrance in the east wall and a fireplace on the north still remain. The irregular heights and sizes of the surviving windows suggest periodic alterations to the rooms when domestic comfort began to take priority over defence, possibly after the subjugation of Wales by 1300.

The polygonal bailey to the north-east of the keep encompasses an area of about 0.04ha and is surrounded by a weak wall standing up to 3m high and approximately 1.5m thick, part of which has a battered base. There are frag-

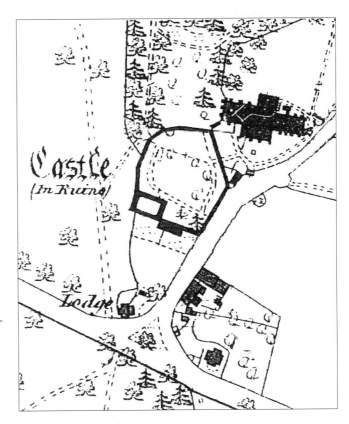

5 Nineteenth-century plan of Alberbury Castle. Note the close proximity of the church

6 The ruined keep at Alberbury, with part of the bailey wall

ments of a tower at its north-west angle. However, the existing wall may not accurately reflect the original perimeter. A map of 1579 does not show a wall and what now stands has been considerably altered, especially to the east and south. It is possible that much of the present curtain wall was restored after the Civil War (its south-east doorway is dated 1646) and that stretches were renovated as part of the landscaping of Loton Park in the eighteenth century. The doorways to the north-west and north-east are nineteenth-century. There are no traces of defensive earthworks or ditches around the keep or bailey.

Apley Castle sj 656132

The date of the construction of the first castle at Apley near Wellington is unknown, but it appears to have originated as a moated mansion which Adam de Charlton was given licence to crenellate by Edward III in 1327. It stood near Home Farm, which lies off the A442 north-east of Wellington.

The castle was rebuilt and restored over generations by the Charlton family, especially in the years after 1600 when over £6,000 was spent on a complete refurbishment by its owner, Thomas Hanmer, who had married into the Charlton family. Parliamentary forces tried to seize Apley late in 1642, such was its importance on the Shrewsbury–Wellington road, but were driven off. In March 1643 Hanmer agreed to accept a Royalist garrison, having been ordered to do so or see the castle blown up, but Apley fell to a sudden Parliamentary attack in March 1644 before it had been put into an adequate state of defence. The castle was badly damaged before it was retaken by Sir William Vaughan and 'the rebells' driven off. Simply to deny the place to the enemy in future, the Royal Commissioners ordered Apley to be 'dismantled' and its lead taken to Shrewsbury Castle.

Although repaired to habitable level, the old castle was abandoned by 1794, parts being retained for use as outbuildings, to a new mansion erected close by. Designed by J.H. Haycock and built largely of brick, its construction began *c.*1780 and it was considerably extended in 1856. Its newer, or garden, facade was built in a mixture of Classical, French and Italian styles, much more elaborate than the earlier Georgian half.

Sadly, the mansion was demolished in 1956 and nothing remains of the original castle, though in surviving outbuildings and garden walls there are

7 The seventeenth-century house at Apley, largely the creation of Thomas Hanmer

masonry fragments dating to the seventeenth and eighteenth centuries. The castle moat is no longer visible, although archaeological investigation has established its location and extent.

Aston Botterell SO 631841 ★

In 1086, the manor of Aston was one of many held by Reginald de Bailleul (Balliol), Sheriff of Shropshire. It later passed to the Fitz Alans and was held (as subtenants) by the Botterell family, from whom the village takes its name. The remains of a ringwork and medieval field boundaries lie on gently sloping land overlooking a tributary of the Moor Brook, 100m west of the twelfth-century church of St Michael. The ringwork is oval, enclosing an area of over 30 x 40m with an internal bank about 6m wide. It is defended by a ditch some 7m wide and by what is now only a low outer bank. Most of the features have been destroyed on the east side, nearest Manor Farm. Earth banks representing later field boundaries are visible to the north and west of the site.

It is possible that the ringwork was replaced as a residence by the thirteenth-century manor Farm, which lies only 50m to its east.

8 Part of the ringwork at Aston Botterell, with Manor Farm and the church in the background

9 The motte at Beguildy, showing part of the bailey banks

Beguildy – The Moat so 188805 **

A fine example of a small motte and bailey stands at The Moat Farm, 1km north-west of Beguildy, on the Welsh border. It occupies a low ridge by a stream which runs along its north-eastern side before turning southwards to join the River Teme.

The steeply-sided motte, which has a summit diameter of about 10m, stands over 7m high, and is surrounded by a ditch which is over 9m wide where it survives. The earth ramparts and ditches of the small D-shaped bailey to the south-east of the mound are equally well preserved, especially on the south-east and south-west sides. The defences along the north-east side of the site are less extensive, perhaps having been eroded away by the stream. Nothing is known of its history.

Belan Bank Motte sj 342200 *

The well-defined motte and bailey at Belan Bank lies beside a stream 250m east of Farm Hall. It is a double motte with no visible surrounding ditch. A roughly

10 The double motte at Belan Bank with the bailey raised in foreground

circular lower platform approximately 2m high carries a smaller motte, 4m high, with a flat summit. It lies at the north side of a raised semicircular bailey platform, which is 1.5m above ground level. Very little remains of a ditch around the bailey, though there are faint traces of one along the southern side of the site.

Its location only 0.5km north of Edgerley and 1km south-east of the church at Kinnerley has led to speculation that the motte may be either the castle of *Eggelawe* or *Kinardslie* (or may relate to both). The former is referred to in 1212-3, during the reign of King John, when Robert de Vipont was appointed Constable and the latter after its capture in a surprise attack by the Welsh under Llewellyn in 1223. There are no other known castles in the area to which these allusions might refer. In the early Middle Ages, *Kenardeleye* was a manor held by the Audleys, with *Egardesley* as one of its 'members'.

Bicton Motte SO 289826

Bicton was a 'member' of the Barony of Clun and formed one element of the Manor of the Five Towns, along with Newcastle (q.v.), Llanhedrick, Whitcott and Keysett. The castle which lies just to the west of Bicton may never have been completed and there is no sign of an associated bailey. The motte appears to have been formed from a natural glacial mound and stands to a height of just over 2m in places. It has been so badly damaged by gravel digging that its original size and shape are not clear; it now resembles an almost circular series of low mounds, lying alongside the River Unk. Its surrounding ditch and bank survive only on the south-east side, where the ditch is up to 10m wide and 2m deep, with the outside bank approximately 1m high and 8m wide.

11 The damaged remains of the motte at Bicton, near Clun

Bicton – The Isle SJ 457167

The area around The Isle farm and Isle Park at Bicton, 5km north-west of Shrewsbury, would seem to lend itself to a defensive use, since it is nearly surrounded by a loop of the Severn. Within the loop, to the west of The Isle farm, lie the remains of a medieval moated site but a circular mound at its south-east corner is considered to be a 'prospect mound' upon which a summerhouse stood rather than an earlier motte.

Binweston Mound SJ 301041

Binweston was an outlier of the large manor of Worthen. An oval mound which stood in the village, which lies off the B4386 3km west of Worthen, has largely been destroyed by building. The *Victoria County History* in 1908 described it as being over 4m high, 15m across its summit and surrounded by a ditch, which was fed by a nearby stream. Only a fragment now survives as a low platform and there is no firm evidence that it was in fact a motte.

Bishop's Castle SO 393891

Bishop's Castle was another Norman foundation on the Welsh border which combined a castle and planned borough. The castle, sometimes known as Lydbury or Lydbury North, after the large Episcopal manor in whose western part it lies, was built by the Bishop of Hereford and presumably replaced the castle at Bishop's Moat (q.v.). In fact, it is not easy to distinguish between references to the two and some of those before *c.*1260 possibly relate to Bishop's Moat.

The motte and bailey may have been built as early as 1100, its shape perhaps reflected in the street pattern of the upper town. The first reference occurs in 1154 when the castle came under Mortimer control but it was back in Episcopal hands under Bishop Foliot in 1155 and shortly afterwards 20 marks were spent on it – possibly the beginning of a refortification in stone. In 1263 the castle (as *Lindeberinort*) was attacked and badly damaged (to a cost of 200 marks) by John Fitz Alan, Earl of Arundel and lord of Oswestry and Clun. In that year, Henry III ordered the bishop to take up residence in his castle of *Ledesbury North* to ensure the defence of the area. A survey of 1281 refers to the 'new' castle and the first references to Bishop's Castle under that name (*Bissopes Castle* or *castrum Episcopi*) occur from 1285.

The castle stood on a south-facing spur, its mound shaped from the top of a hill, with the town laid out below it along a central road running towards the Norman church of St John. The castle and church thus marked the north–south limits of the borough (*colour plate 24*). Little is known of its history in the Middle Ages but it seems to have been in good repair throughout its existence, bearing in mind that it also served as a Bishop's Palace and a regional administrative centre. As late as *c.*1540, Leland referred to it as 'well menteined on a steep rock not very hy' and of 'good strength'. A survey in the late sixteenth century equally records that it was in good condition and mentions 13 rooms covered with lead, a number of towers, a 'new building', two rooms covered with tiles, a prison tower, stable, dovecote, gardens and park.

In 1603 James I granted the castle to the Howard family and in 1618 it was acquired, together with the ancient Honour of Clun, by the Earl of Arundel. The last reference to an appointment of a Constable at the castle dates to 1610 and from then on it seems to have gone into decline. Somewhat strangely for such a locally significant castle, it does not feature in accounts of the Civil War and there is no mention of its slighting. The town seems to have been divided

12 Nineteenth-century print of Bishop's Castle based on an earlier drawing. Although perhaps somewhat elongated, it appears to be an accurate representation of the large castle which has just about completely vanished

13 The only surviving freestanding fragment of the castle walls of Bishop's Castle

in its loyalties during the war, but though a Royalist attack in September 1644 burned parts of the town and Parliamentary cavalry were stationed in the church in 1645, there is no sign that the castle was in use.

One assumes that over years, as at other urban sites (like Wem and Oswestry), its stone and materials were sold or removed for re-use elsewhere. Fragments of the structure recorded in the nineteenth century and as late as 1940 no longer survive and hardly anything of this important castle now remains visible. The mound on which the keep stood has been lowered and levelled and is now occupied by a bowling green but its slope may be seen rising from the gardens of the adjacent Castle Hotel. Most of the bailey lies under the hotel and nearby buildings but its perimeter line is preserved in the surrounding street plan. It stretched southwards into the town to the area occupied by The Square. There are sections of walls, a blocked gateway and other stonework built into various buildings nearby, but these are not usually open to view. An angled section of the bailey's shale curtain wall some 10m long by 2.5m high – the sole free-standing remnant of the castle's structure – stands to the west of the castle mound.

Bishop's Moat so 291896 **

Near a farm on the Shropshire–Powys border, 3.25km north-west of Bishop's Castle, is a large earthwork known as Bishop's Moat. Sited to control the Kerry Ridgeway, an important east–west route, it is still very impressive, its large mound surrounded by a well-defined ditch and with clearly identifiable bailey perimeters. The gorse-covered motte has a base diameter of approximately 37m and stands to a height of over 5m, surrounded by a deep ditch more than 10m wide in places. The oval bailey is defended by a wide earth bank up to 2m high, its entrance lying to the east, near the modern farm (*colour plate 20*).

The castle was probably built *c.*1100 and occurs early in its history as 'Lydbury' or 'Lydbury North', after the manor held by the Bishops of Hereford. Little is known about it and early references to the castle of Lydbury North could refer to Bishop's Moat or Bishop's Castle (q.v.). It may have been abandoned in the mid-thirteenth century, succeeded by Bishop's Castle as the main Episcopal residence and fortification in the area.

14 An aerial view of the fine motte and bailey castle at Bishop's Moat on the Kerry Ridgeway. The road from Bishop's Castle is visible at the top. *CPAT*

Blakemere Castle SJ 560425

About 1km north-east of Whitchurch, on the south side of Blakemere Pool, is a roughly square, moated site representing all that remains of the 'castle' of the Talbots, Earls of Shrewsbury, who acquired Blakemere in the late fourteenth century from its original owners, the le Strange family. The site may be that of the mansion in *Whitecherche* which Fulke le Strange received licence to crenellate in 1322; both the house and a park are referred to in 1361. It remained in occupation to be described by Leland in the 1540s as 'the large park of Blakemere belonging to the Earl of Shrewsbury, wherein a very fair place or lodge'. The Talbots sold the manor in 1590 and it is possible that the house was damaged during the Civil War, since in the late 1690s it was described as a ruin.

The platform, extending to approximately 54 x 52m, rises up to 2m above the surrounding ground and stands within the remains of a wide moat, now

15 The platform at Blakemere, showing the damaged west side

dry, which averages about 10m in width where it survives. The interior is level but bears the scars of archaeological excavations in 1963, particularly on the north side. On its west side the island has been partially quarried away and the moat filled in. The other arms of the moat survive but those to the north-east and south-east have been reduced by ploughing. At the west end of the north-west arm what may be an original causeway approximately 5m wide runs to the lake, presumably to a landing place on that side.

Bretchel Motte SJ 337117

Bretchel does not occur in Domesday Book, though *Bredeshull* was later part of the holdings of the Corbets of Caus. 'The Beacon', lying 100m south-west of the farm at Bretchel, is a steep-sided, isolated, tree-capped motte. It stands in open farmland on the top of a south-facing slope with excellent views over the surrounding area and over the Shrewsbury–Welshpool road. The area is dotted with motte and bailey castles whose function was presumably to control this important route.

The small, largely circular mound has a base diameter of approximately 15m and stands 3m above the surrounding land. Faint remains of a surrounding ditch are still visible, but all traces of its bailey, which may have lain to the south-east of the motte, have now gone.

16 The wind-swept motte at Bretchel

Bridgnorth Castle SO 717927 ★★

Bridgnorth lay in the Saxon manor of *Membrefelde* (later Morville), part of which was in the hands of Earl Roger in 1086. A Norman castle was built there *c.*1101 by Roger's son, Robert of Bellême (*c.*1054-1131), 3rd Earl of Shrewsbury, who transferred to Bridgnorth the church from his father's foundation at Quatford. He clearly recognised the superior defensive and strategic potential of the high sandstone promontory overlooking the Severn and constructed a new castle, probably in earth and timber, on the south end of the spur. Orderic Vitalis records that during his rebellion in 1102, Robert withdrew to Bridgnorth 'where he was building a very strong castle ... on the River Severn'. Henry I besieged and captured the castle which, following the forfeiture of Earl Robert's estates, was eventually given to Hugh de Mortimer. However, Mortimer proved to be an equally unreliable vassal and on his accession in 1154 Henry II requested the surrender of Mortimer's castles at Bridgnorth, Wigmore and Cleobury. When this was refused, Henry attacked Bridgnorth in 1155 and captured the castle. Large sums were spent on the now royal castle between 1168-89, creating a powerful stone fortress whose fragmentary remains survive.

Principal amongst them is a massive square keep constructed *c.*1170 standing at the north end of a stone-walled inner bailey. The outer bailey extended northwards towards the town and in 1211-2 King John added a powerful

17 The remains of the Norman keep at Bridgnorth from the inner bailey side

barbican or gateway defence, whose remains were discovered in 1821 near the old Post Office. In the early thirteenth century the whole town was surrounded by earth ramparts and ditches which, from the 1260s, were replaced by stone walls and gateways. As early as 1281, however, the castle was reported to be dilapidated and although repairs were undertaken by Edward I (who was in Bridgnorth in 1294 and 1295) its military function declined with the conquest of Wales by 1300. The castle was occupied by Edward II in 1321 and later by Henry IV but was clearly allowed to fall into decay. By the time of Leland's visit in the 1540s, the castle was in a poor state of repair, with houses encroaching into the outer bailey and the great gateway blocked up.

In the early seventeenth century, the castle was sold to the Whitmore family of nearby Apley. Made defensible for the Civil War, it was visited by Charles I in 1642 and 1645 and defended by Sir Robert Howard when besieged by Parliamentary forces in 1646. Digging into its sandstone base, they threatened to undermine and blow up the castle, forcing its garrison to surrender after 26 days of siege in April 1646. Parliament almost immediately ordered the destruction of the castle and the result is the present shattered ruin of the great keep, destroyed by gunpowder and left to lean at the seemingly impossible angle of 15 degrees – greater than the Tower of Pisa!

The keep, faced with grey limestone, has typical pilaster buttresses and measured 12.5 x 11.5m, standing to a height of about 22m. It was entered (as was usual) from the first floor and stood in the middle of the north side of the inner bailey wall, fragments of which remain nearby, close to its gateway. The tower presents a bleakly defensive external face, especially on the more vulnerable north side, where its walls are nearly 3m thick and lack any slits or openings. As was common, its lowest floor was an unlit storeroom, with a hall above. Little remains of any internal features apart from a latrine chamber in the west wall and fragments of a fireplace on the south. A further floor contained a bedroom or rooms and above that, a sloping roof was surrounded by battlements, now gone. The inner bailey is defined by the modern public garden and is surrounded on all sides except the north, where the outer bailey stood, by high sandstone cliffs. The height allows a commanding view over the Severn, its important bridge and the surrounding area.

The outer bailey to the north is now built over, largely occupied by Georgian houses around the church of St Mary Magdalene. Reconstructed by Thomas Telford in 1792, this was originally the castle chapel and lay within its perimeters (*colour plate 2*). Beyond that lay the town itself. Of the town walls, only hidden fragments remain, incorporated into later buildings, and of the town's five gates only the North Gate remains and this was largely rebuilt in 1910.

The earthwork known as Pan Pudding Hill (*colour plate 32*), which stands on a hillside only 500m south-west of the castle, is believed to have been built as a siege work by Henry I in 1102 or by Henry II in 1155. It was certainly used as such during the Civil War, becoming a gun-emplacement during the siege of 1646 when Parliamentary artillery pounded the castle for 26 days. The earthwork is 55m in diameter, with an earth-covered gravel and stone rampart rising to about 3m above the outside ground level. A narrow bailey stretches to its west, separated from the fort by a shallow ditch.

Broadward Motte so 394766

In 1086, Broadward was held by the de Hopton family amongst their Hopton estates. The tree-covered, elongated motte lies in the grounds of Broadward

18 The castle mound at Broadward on the River Clun

Hall, standing on the banks of the River Clun which runs along its eastern side. Like those at Clungunford and Leintwardine, the castle would have controlled crossing points on the lower section of the river. The sloping mound stands some 3m high at its north-western end, rising to 3.5m at the southeast. The summit measures about 18 x 10m, its deformed shape explained by the fact that the motte was once considered to be a burial mound and was dug into, without result, to investigate its interior. There are no traces of a surrounding ditch or of any bailey features, which presumably have been eroded away or silted up by the periodic flooding of the river over centuries.

Brockhurst Castle SO 446925 ★★

Brockhurst Castle is a fascinating site, with well-preserved ditches, banks and bailey platforms. But what looks like a typical earth and timber castle was in fact a royal fortress with a probable tower keep and stone curtain walls. It lies at the southern end of a ridge overlooking the marshy Stretton Dale, opposite Little Stretton, and is believed to have been built by Henry II *c*.1154 to control part of the important Ludlow-Shrewsbury route.

The castle has a complicated but brief history, covering only a century *c*.1154-5. After its construction around 1154–1255, custody was given to Engelhard de Pitchford, who later assumed the surname 'de Stretton' and held it until *c.*1175. Repairs were carried out in 1194-5 under Richard I, but its ownership was later disputed between its custodian Hugh de Neville and John Fitz Alan. Fitz Alan seized the castle illegally in 1212, remaining in occupation until 1215 when he was forced to relinquish control. It may have suffered serious damage in the process. Brockhurst passed to Hugh de Burgh in 1229 and, following his fall in 1232, was given in 1238 to Henry of Hastings, who is known to have carried out repairs. However, Brockhurst seems to have been abandoned as early as 1255 when a survey stated that there was no castle in Stretton.

The earthworks consist of two high, flat baileys, 6-8m above ground level, separated by a massive ditch some 12m wide and 3m deep. The north-east bailey is approximately 42 x 26m, with the remains of an earth rampart 0.5m high on its west and east sides. What is probably the original entrance cuts through the rampart on the north side, where a trackway approaches the castle from the north-west and crosses the ditch.

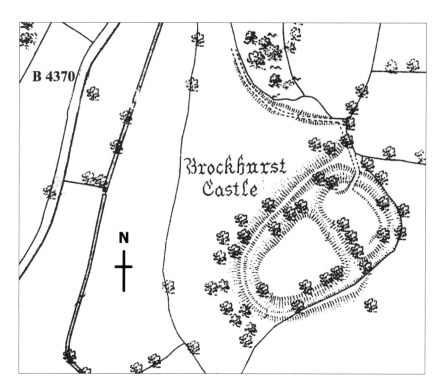

19 Plan of Brockhurst Castle

20 The high platform and part of the ditch of the southern bailey at Brockhurst

The south-western bailey is larger (at approximately 52 x 40m) and about 1m higher than the northern bailey. It was defended by a rampart and excavation on its north-west side in 1959 showed it to have carried a strong shale wall. The excavation also revealed signs of timber buildings within the baileys and indicated that they were joined by a wooden bridge crossing the ditch.

Both baileys are surrounded by an impressive ditch, up to 10m wide, with an outer bank remaining on all but the east side. Fragments of the castle's stonework were visible into the early nineteenth century but have since been robbed away and only small pieces are scattered around the site or protrude from the ground.

Brockton Motte SO 580933

At the time of Domesday, Brockton was held of the powerful Rainald (or Reginald), Sheriff of Shropshire, by one Richard. The manor later passed to the Fitz Alans and was held of them by the de Brockton family.

The castle lies in gardens 250m east of the crossroads in Brockton. The tree-covered motte is a well-defined oval mound approximately 25 x 20m,

21 Part of the low motte and flooded ditch at Brockton

rising over 2m above its surrounding ditch. This is clearly visible to the east but the western section is now flooded as part of a large pond, as is the bailey which lay in that area. A bank running for approximately 60m to the north probably marks the bailey's boundary in that direction, though it may have been heightened to form part of the pond dam. A fast-flowing stream runs on the north of the site, along the present road towards Weston.

Brogyntyn Castle SJ 274314

The ringwork known as 'Castell Brogyntyn' is traditionally assigned to Brogyntyn, son of Prince Owen Madre of Powis, who died *c.*1205, and may have been intended to counter the Norman works at Oswestry. It stands on a site of great natural strength – a spur high above the surrounding land – in the parkland of Brogyntyn Hall, 300m north-east of Brogyntyn Farm. The site is very impressive in its location and scale but is so completely overgrown with trees and bushes that it is impossible to gain an overall view.

The interior has a diameter of some 45m, bounded by an earth rampart up to 2m high, and stands over 5m above a wide surrounding ditch, around which are remnants of an earth bank. The entrance seems to have been to the north-east of the site.

The top of the mound, which is equally overgrown, was levelled for use as a bowling green in modern times and the remains of a brick structure in the north-west bank probably relate to this use. An unusual feature at Brogyntyn is an 80m tunnel, 2m high, which passes right underneath the site from north-west to south-east. Its function is unknown, but it may have been a landscape feature to add interest to a walk through Brogyntyn park and towards the ornamental lakes which the castle now overlooks.

Bromfield SO 479769

There is little to suggest that a castle ever existed at Bromfield, 3.5km north-west of Ludlow. However, Leland recorded that 'there is liklyhod that the castle of Bromfield, belonged to Giffard, and by force razed, stood where now is a farmhouse moated belonging to the Earl of Oxford'. A square, moated site certainly survives as an earthwork, with a few fragments of stonework representing its former buildings. It may have been nothing more than a grange of the ancient Bromfield Priory, a daughter-house of Gloucester Abbey.

Bromlow Motte SJ 320024

The motte lying between Betton and Bromlow is one of a cluster dotted along the valley of the Rea Brook and part of the series occupying the Rea–Camlad gap. Carved out of the natural rock on the northern side of a high, steep spur, a bank separates it from the adjoining land to its south. The site lies between two tributaries of the Rea Brook and has commanding views to its north, where it overlooks the Shrewsbury–Montgomery route. The rocky nature of the site dictates the size of the mound, which is now approximately 4.5m high with a rounded, eroded summit about 8m in diameter. It is surrounded by a ditch, which is up to 1m deep and visible on all sides except the east where the ground slopes steeply away.

There are no traces of a bailey, which may have lain in the area now covered by Village Farm, which is immediately adjacent to the south-east side of the motte. Less than 1km to the north-east lies Whitsburn Hill (q.v.).

22 The castle mound at Bromlow from the north

Brompton Motte SO 251931

In 1086, the manor of Brompton was held of Earl Roger by Picot de Say, with a smaller part recorded as 'waste' held by Roger Fitz Corbet. Around 1095 Picot granted its tithes to Shrewsbury Abbey and his successor, Henry de Say, lord of Clun, exchanged Brompton for Cheney Longville, which was one of the Abbey's holdings. Brompton remained in the hands of Shrewsbury Abbey until its dissolution in 1539.

The tree-covered motte stands behind a public house on the crossroads of the A489 with the B4385 and adjacent to Brompton Mill, whose buildings encroach into the east and south of the site. The castle lay right on Offa's Dyke, running only a few metres to its west, and may have controlled a crossing of the Caebitra stream, the modern boundary between England and Wales, which runs immediately to the south of the castle.

The circular, steep-sided mound is very large, 30m in diameter at its base, rising to a flat summit 9m in diameter. Its surrounding ditch is clearly defined, up to 2m deep and over 7m wide in places. The bailey was roughly triangular and lay to the south-east of the mound. Much of its perimeter has been ploughed away, but traces of its bank remain, especially to the south, though the bailey ditch itself is now largely filled in.

23 The motte at Brompton

Broncroft Castle SO 545867 ★

The castle of Broncroft survives as an attractive nineteenth-century country house which retains little of its medieval structure, apart from an adapted fourteenth-century tower to the right of the main entrance.

Broncroft was a 'member' of the manor of Corfham and descended in the de Clifford family. Lying near a stream in Corvedale, 1km west of Tugford and close to Corfham (q.v.), the castle is thought to have been built by Roger Tyrell in the early fourteenth century. It passed to the Burley family in the 1360s and the earliest surviving parts of the present building may be the work of Simon Burley c.1380. Burley, an important figure in the household of Edward III's son, the Black Prince, was disgraced and executed in 1386. Nevertheless, his family retained ownership of Broncroft until the mid-fifteenth century when it passed via various hands to the Talbots, the Earls of Shrewsbury. In the 1540s, Leland refers to 'Bramscrofte, a very goodly place like a castel, longing to the Erle of Shrewsbiri'.

By the end of the sixteenth century, Broncroft was held by the Lutley family of Enville. Under John Lutley it was garrisoned for the King until June 1645 when, like other Shropshire castles, it appears to have been slighted by its garrison when they withdrew. It is recorded as 'taken' by a Parliamentary

24 Broncroft Castle: the square tower (centre) is one of the few remnants of the medieval castle

force from Shrewsbury in June 1645 and a contemporary report declared that 'Braincroft' was 'much demolished' so the new Parliamentary garrison 'fell to repaire and fortify it'. The castle was attacked by Royalists under Sir William Vaughan on 4 July 1645 and a severe action was fought nearby, but Broncroft did not fall. The castle was deliberately damaged when the Parliamentary garrison withdrew at the end of the war and further slighted by order of Parliament in July 1648.

The Lutley family repaired what was left of their home between *c*.1660-80, though not apparently in any grand style, and it remained in their possession until 1807. Much of the present 'castle' was built by the Johnstone family in the early nineteenth century and by James Whitaker, who bought the house in 1889 and gave it what Pevsner called a 'picturesquely asymmetrical appearance'.

Bryn Amlwg Castle SO 167846 ★★

Castell Bryn Amlwg ('the castle on a prominent hill'), near Bettws-y-Crwyn, was built on a well-chosen site. Lying in marshy land close to Offa's Dyke, it stands on an oval platform at the south-western point of a spur of Cefn Fron Hill and is also known as Castell Cefn Fron. It dominates the Rhuddwr valley and has commanding views in all directions except the east, where it is overlooked by higher ground.

The castle lies in the Forest of Clun and presumably served as an outpost on the Welsh border of the Barony of Clun. It also occupies a strategic location south of the Kerry Ridgeway, an important route into mid-Wales from Bishop's Castle. The builder of the original castle is unknown, but it was presumably one of the de Say family as lords of Clun in the twelfth century.

Unusually for an early Shropshire castle, Bryn Amlwg has received some archaeological investigation in the form a series of digs in 1963. These revealed a complicated history of construction and development and despite its present appearance as an impressive range of earthworks and ditches, at its height in the thirteenth century Bryn Amlwg was a substantial stone castle.

It appears to have originated in the twelfth century as a ringwork, probably carrying a wooden palisade, with wooden internal buildings. This was

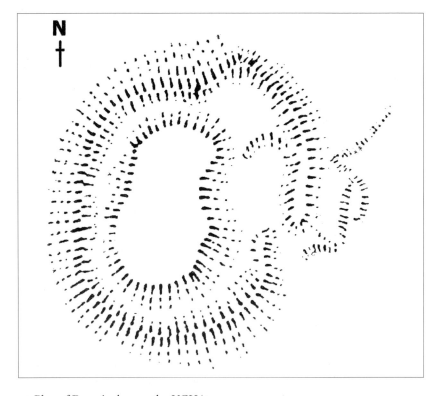

25 Plan of Bryn Amlwg castle. *VCH/1*

26 The site at Bryn Amlwg from the south, showing the outer rampart and inner motte

infilled to create an oval motte, now approximately 30 x 48m across its summit and about 6m high, with the remains of ramparts around its perimeter. It is surrounded by a deep, steep-sided ditch which is further protected by an earth bank up to 4m high in places and which may have carried stone walls. At a later stage, stone walls were built around the motte and a circular tower constructed on its south-west side. A D-shaped stone tower was built more or less in the centre of each of the western and eastern curtain walls and a strong gatehouse, defended by twin towers, was incorporated into the northern end. The collapsed stonework of these and other structures lies under the surface of the mound and in the ditch. The main entrance to the site was to the north, where there is a break in the rampart opposite the site of the gatehouse.

It is difficult to establish who built which phase of the castle, since there are few historical references to the site. The ringwork was probably the work of Helias de Say in the mid-twelfth century and intended to defend the western borders of his estates. The first stone reconstruction may have been carried out in the mid-thirteenth century by John Fitz Alan, as lord of Clun, and included the round tower to the south and the curtain walls. Some of the later strengthening of the site (e.g. the northern gatehouse) may have been carried out by the Welsh prince Llewellyn ap Gruffydd *c.*1260-70 or it may represent the further development of the castle by the Fitz Alans at a time of conflict with Wales. It is unlikely that the Bryn Amlwg remained in use much beyond the end of the Welsh campaigns *c.*1300.

The eastern side of the site has been mutilated by quarrying in former years, which has breached the outer rampart and widened the ditch in that area.

Bucknell Motte SO 355739

At the time of Domesday, the manor of Bucknell was held by Ralph Mortimer, son of Roger de Mortemer, Steward of Earl Roger. Ralph received a number of estates which fell forfeit to the king following the rebellion of 1074 and his lands in Shropshire and Herefordshire eventually formed the Barony of Wigmore, one of the great Marcher lordships. From Ralph Mortimer, Bucknell was one of a number of holdings of Helgot, formerly tenant of Roger of Montgomery and the builder of Holdgate castle (q.v.).

The small, damaged motte at Bucknell lies on a farm approximately 150m north-east of the church of St Mary, in water meadows lying along the north bank of the River Redlake. It may have controlled a crossing on the river, which is now little more than a narrow stream. Although the tree-capped motte still stands to a height of approximately 3m, with a summit 7.5m across and base diameter of approximately 46m, much of it has been cut away to the north and north-west by farm buildings and an ice-house was built into its north-west face. Traces of a ditch are visible around the base of the motte to the north-east.

27 The eroded remains of the motte at Bucknell

A few weapons believed to date to the Civil War have been found on the site, though nothing is known of its re-use at that time.

Burford Motte SO 594686

The extensive manor of Burford has an interesting early history. In 1086, it was held by Osbern, son of the Norman lord Richard Scrope (*le Scrob*), the builder of Richard's Castle, who was given extensive holdings on the Herefordshire–Shropshire border by Edward the Confessor *c*.1050 – i.e. before the Norman conquest. The early Norman castles at Burford, Homme and Richard's Castle, part of a chain of defences along the Teme, are an interesting example of the early employment of Norman lords in vulnerable areas on the Welsh frontier. Much of the territory given to Richard had been laid waste by Welsh depredations over many years and it was clearly his function to stabilise the area. By the time of Domesday, Richard, who may have built Burford castle as early as *c*.1055, had been succeeded by his son Osbern, who made Burford the principal residence or *caput* of his Shropshire lands. Most of the Scrope estates were incorporated into the Honour of Richard's Castle and the manor of Burford later passed to the Mortimer family.

28 The castle mound at Burford, opposite the crossing of the Teme at Tenbury Wells. It may be the earliest Norman motte in Shropshire

A clearly defined motte stands on the flood plain of the Teme at Burford, on the Shropshire side of the bridge at Tenbury Wells, and was presumably constructed to command the river crossing. There is little to see apart from the mound, rising to approximately 3.5m, with a summit diameter of 4m, standing on a slightly raised platform. There are faint indications of a causeway leading to the castle at its north-eastern edge. However, all traces of a bailey, banks and ditches have gone, presumably eroded away or silted up by the river over generations.

Callow Hill sj 384049

Standing 2km south-west of Pontesbury, Callow Hill, topped with a circular copse of trees, is one of the most distinctive landmarks in the area. In the trees lies a small, triangular Iron Age hill-fort, with two well-preserved ramparts enclosing a space of about 0.3ha, entered via a causeway on its north-east side.

It has been suggested that this fort was re-used as the basis for a stone castle, just as Ritton and Caus had adapted existing earthworks. A castle at Callow, apparently built by the Corbets of Caus, is referred to in the 1270s and Leland reported masonry remains on the site. However, there is now no evidence for a medieval castle and nothing has been found to suggest that one existed on this spot.

29 Callow Hill, with its distinctive copse of trees: the location of an Iron Age fort apparently adapted as a later castle

Castle Pulverbatch SJ 423022 ★★★

In 1086 Pulverbatch, now divided into Castle Pulverbatch and Church Pulverbatch, was one large vill and one of six manors held of Earl Roger by Roger 'the Hunter' (*Venator*). It was the *caput* or centre of the Barony of Pulverbatch by the end of the twelfth century and it is possible that the adjacent village was a planned settlement, laid out alongside the castle in the twelfth or thirteenth centuries.

Roger Hunter presumably built the impressive motte and bailey castle. Superbly sited to control the ancient Shrewsbury–Bishop's Castle route, it commands extensive views to its south and is defended on that side by a steep slope falling 30m to the stream below. The castle, first referred to *c.*1135, passed through various hands before 1250 – the Pulverbatch, de Castello, Kilpeck, Cantilupe and Marmion familes. Still occupied *c.*1205, there are sporadic references to the castle into the fourteenth century, though by then a domestic use had presumably overtaken any military or defensive function; its chapel is mentioned as late as 1427.

The circular motte has a summit diameter of approximately 36.5m and stands to a height of 8.5m above a steep natural slope on its south-eastern side. A wide ditch, 2.5m deep, defends its north-east and west sides. The equally impressive inner bailey, 37 x 18m, lies to the north-east of the motte and is defended by an

30 An aerial view of the impressive motte and baileys at Castle Pulverbatch, the outer bailey at the top of the photograph. *CPAT-92-MB-419*

31 View of the main motte at Pulverbatch (right), its deep surrounding ditch (left) and its raised north-east bailey

earth rampart rising to 1.5m above the interior and over 4m above the outer bailey; its wide surrounding ditch is over 1m deep. To the west of the motte is a semicircular outer bailey, possibly a later addition, defended by a bank over 1m high on its west and a scarp over 2m high on the south. It has a modern entrance on its north-west side. There do not appear to have been any stone buildings on the site, which perhaps remained as an earth and timber structure over the comparatively long period of its existence.

Caus Castle sj 337078 ★★★

Caus (or Cause) was one of many outliers of the ancient manor of Worthen. This large manor was given to the Corbet family and by the time of Domesday was one of 30 held of Earl Roger by Roger Corbet. Probably in the mid-twelfth century the family built the castle at Caus, which became the centre of the powerful Barony of Caus. Its name recalls the Pays de Caux, the Corbet homeland in Normandy. The ringwork at Hawcock's Mount (q.v.), only 1km to the east, may have been a predecessor to Caus, its name being a corruption of *Aldecause* or 'old Cause'.

Caus was probably the creation of Roger Corbet (d.1134) and is first referred to in 1140, apparently having been burned by the Welsh in 1134. After briefly passing into royal ownership it reverted to the Corbets by 1175, but such was its importance to the defence of the Welsh frontier that Robert Corbet received 10 marks from the King for repairs in 1198 and his successors received further sums in 1225 and in 1263. Caus passed to the de Leybournes in the fourteenth century and in 1347 to the Staffords; in 1399 large amounts were spent on the tower near the gate, the stretch of wall 'between Grumbaldeston (tower) and the bakehouse' and other towers which were in a poor state of repair.

The castle was garrisoned during the revolt by Owain Glyndwr in the early fifteenth century but seems to have been abandoned as a residence by the Staffords shortly afterwards. It did, however, retain some use as an administrative centre and prison. By 1521, the castle was 'in grete ruine and decay' and not until the 1540s and 1550s were extensive repairs undertaken by lord Henry Stafford, who built a new house in the bailey; this may be represented by the rectangular hall site whose footings are still visible. By 1573 under the Thynne family – the builders of Longleat – the castle was again in decay, but between 1630-40 the considerable sum of £800 was spent on renovation and repair. All was destroyed as early as 1645 when the castle was slighted by order of Parliament.

Whatever its state in 1642, Caus must have remained an imposing site. It was then owned by Sir Henry Thynne and was put into a state of defence early in the war. It remained in Royalist hands under Captain Davalier, a Florentine mercenary, until June 1645 when a force from Shrewsbury attacked the castle. The garrison of 300 initially refused to surrender, but 'after seven days' siege' capitulated on the 25 June and was allowed to march to Ludlow. The castle appears to have been slighted immediately afterwards. Sir Henry Thynne, in Ludlow at the time of his castle's capture, was later imprisoned in Shrewsbury and fined nearly £2,000. He was still in prison in The Fleet as late as 1652, his family ruined by their losses.

The castle adapted what was probably an Iron Age hill-fort standing on a ridge of the Long Mountain which towers over 50m above Rea Brook valley. It is one of the most impressive defensive positions in the area, dominating the Montgomery–Shrewsbury route. Although the lower site at Hawcock's gave more immediate access to the valley route, Caus offered a commanding view of the area to the east, west and south. The circular motte and the inner bailey to its north-east lie within the massive double ramparts and deep ditches of the existing fort, now shrouded with trees and undergrowth. The outer bailey lay in the field to the north, beyond the hill-fort's ramparts, and was occupied by a small town, the borough of Caus (see below). This was encircled by a stone curtain wall with towers by about 1300 and two defended gates, the East Gate and the South West or Wallop Gate, gave access to the town.

The large, conical motte stands to a height of over 15m above a ditch approximately 3m deep and over 15m wide. Its narrow summit, with a diameter of approximately 12m, bears a fragment of a circular or D-shaped shale wall, possibly the remains of a shell keep or (more probably) a single tower; the latter is indicated in an early but undated sketch of the castle.

The inner bailey, extending to approximately 70 x 42m and enclosing about 0.35ha, was surrounded by a stone wall, of which only shale fragments remain, set on top of the earlier earth ramparts and further protected by their existing ditches. It was entered via a strongly-defended gatehouse to its north-east. The overgrown ruins of its two D-shaped towers (which controlled the drawbridge access across the outer ditch) and a barbican are still visible. Within the bailey, on its south-eastern side, are the foundations of a large rectangular building, probably the hall and, nearer the foot of the motte lies a deep stone-lined well.

32 An aerial view of the site at Caus. The castle and defences lay in the trees to the centre right and the borough in the field to its left. The position of the town walls is clearly defined in this photo. *CPAT-85-MB-14*

33 Part of the castle mound (left) and the deep ditches and banks formed by the original hill fort defences

In the fields to the north of the castle, effectively its outer bailey, a walled town once stood. It was probably integral to the castle from its earliest days, since it existed by *c.*1200 when the borough was granted the right to hold a weekly market. By 1300 the town was surrounded by a stone wall with 2 gateways and 58 burgage plots were recorded in 1349. However, the town declined from the mid-fourteenth century, possibly as a result of the Black Death or of simple economics and the fact that it was too remote to flourish. It dwindled away in the shadow of the castle, the last mention of a tenanted house occurring in 1614. The chapel of St Margaret, founded in the castle in 1272, is last mentioned in 1447 but the Free Chapel of St Nicholas which stood opposite the castle gate existed until the slighting of the castle in 1645. The main street between East Gate and Wallop Gate was in use as a trackway as late as 1816 though all remains of the houses and other buildings were gone by then.

The remnants of the town walls and gates, the ruins of which were recorded in a watercolour of *c.*1777 by William Williams, were removed in the early nineteenth century to provide road-making material. Today, little remains of the town apart from the faint traces of building platforms which can still be seen,

34 The tree-covered motte at Caus, with fragments of a stone tower on its summit

35 Remains of the south-west or Wallop Gate – the only standing fragment of the town walls of Caus

the deep holloway leading into it from the south-west, a stone fragment of the south-west gate and the scars left by the removal of the walls. At their height in the thirteenth century, the castle and the town together must have been an impressive sight and with its massive earth ramparts and deep ditches, Caus remains one of the most interesting and imposing castle sites in the county.

Charlton Castle SJ 597112

Despite its name, Charlton is better described as a moated manor house. In 1316 it was the home of Sir John de Cherleton who received licence to crenellate from Edward II and it had its own chapel by 1341. The house was occupied by the same family into the mid-sixteenth century but by *c.*1590 it seems to have fallen into disuse. By tradition, it was altered or rebuilt many times.

The site lies in open farmland and survives as a clearly-defined, raised rectangular platform of approximately 50 x 68m. It is surrounded by a wide moat

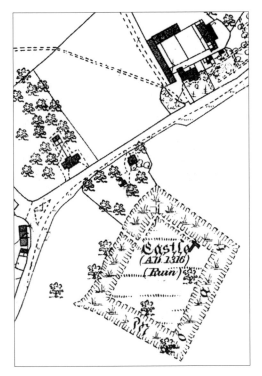

36 A Victorian plan of the moated mansion or castle at Charlton

which is still waterlogged, except for its north-west arm, where the castle's entrance via a narrow causeway remains visible. A large rectangular fishpond lies in the field to the south-east. Significant parts of the castle walling remained in the early nineteenth century and (decreasingly) into the early years of the twentieth. Today, although the layout of its interior structures is traceable, with fragments of sandstone walls around the perimeter of the platform, the whole site is so completely overgrown that it is difficult to gain any clear impression.

Cheney Longville SO 417848 ★★

Longville was held of Earl Roger by Siward 'the fat', its tenant before 1066. The son of Aethelgar, he may have been related to Edward the Confessor and held other manors in Shropshire. Siward is believed to have given the site of Shrewsbury Abbey to Earl Roger in exchange for Cheney Longville. However, Siward later gave Cheney Longville to Shrewsbury Abbey, which exchanged it with Henry de Say of Clun for the manor of Brompton. Cheney Longville then descended in the Fitz Alan Barony of Clun and was held by the de Cheney family by the early fourteenth century.

Ringwork
To the north-west of the village, at a fork in the road, stands 'Castle Ring', an eroded ringwork. It measures approximately 56 x 32m, with a single earth rampart standing up to 2.5m high. Traces of its surrounding ditch are visible on all sides, except the east where roadworks and the construction of a house have damaged the site. Entrances cut through the rampart to its north and south may be modern and there is no trace of an associated bailey.

The ringwork is thought to date to the late eleventh or early twelfth century and is presumably the predecessor of the stone castle which stands only 200m to its south-west (see below). Local tradition claims it as a Civil War siege work intended for operations against the castle – a function it could have performed.

Castle
The stone castle at Cheney Longville is a fascinating site and, all things considered, a remarkably complete survival. The manor passed to the de Cheney family in the early fourteenth century and in 1395 Roger Cheney was granted

37 Part of the low bank of the ringwork at Cheney Longville

by Richard II licence to crenellate his house, though no crenellations remain. It is, in effect, a fortified, moated manor house rather than a more heavily-defended 'castle'.

The main structure comprises a series of four ranges built around an oblong courtyard, entered by an archway through the north-west wing where a stone bridge crosses what remains of the ditch. The main residence, the present farmhouse at the west end of the northern range, stands on the base of the original building. It dates mainly from the sixteenth and seventeenth centuries, with later remodelling and has a veranda with nineteenth-century Tuscan columns. The three ranges on the west, south and east of the courtyard are narrow, two-storeyed buildings, many of whose external medieval features – windows and doorways – still survive in an evocative setting (*colour plate 21*). The walls of the 'castle' are comparatively weak, less than 1m thick in most cases, and there were no towers offering additional height or flank protection to the walls. However, the site was originally surrounded by banks and large moats which would have added an extra protective barrier. The moats survive only as weed-filled, boggy areas to the south and east of the buildings, the other sections having been largely filled in.

To the immediate north-east of the castle are the dry remains of a very large pond, formed by a massive earthen dam, 100m long and 10m wide; this

38 The outer wall of the west range of Cheney Longville, with its original fourteenth-century slits

39 View of the castle at Cheney Longville from the north, across the site of the large lake which lay to its front

lake and the other water features around the site would have considerably enhanced the appearance of the castle in its heyday.

The castle remained in Cheney hands until the mid-fifteenth century when it passed to the Plowdens and from them to the Beddoes family in the eighteenth century. It is believed to have suffered some damage by Parliamentary forces in the Civil War. Many of the farm buildings near the castle are of considerable antiquity, some perhaps as old as the original house.

Cheswardine Castle sj 719301

In 1086, the Staffordshire manor of Cheswardine and Chipnall was held by Robert of Stafford. The manor passed to Henry I and then to the le Strange family in 1160, by which time the area had become part of Shropshire. The manor remained in the hands of the le Strange's until the death of John le Strange in 1330.

The family was presumably responsible for the construction of the 'castle' at Cheswardine, which even by 1330 on the death of John le Strange, was described as being of little strength. What remains is a fine moated site, lying in a woodland plantation approximately 150m north of the church of St Swithin, on the highest land north of the village. The low platform is surrounded by a 20m-wide, water-filled moat, which bulges out on its south-west arm. There are causeways, possibly modern, crossing the south and north arms. Nothing remains of any stonework on the platform, which may have carried only timber buildings.

40 The moated site at Cheswardine

At Castle Ditches Field, 1km east of the village, was another moated site which, given its name, may have been the location for some form of fortification. However, this was extensively damaged by gravel workings and was entirely levelled in 1984 so nothing remains visible today.

Chirbury SO 258985

The manor of Chirbury, a royal estate before 1066, became one of Earl Roger's personal holdings and passed to the de Salnervilles, possibly after the rebellion of 1102. By the late twelfth century it was in the hands of the de Boulers and reverted to the Crown around 1220.

Traditional references to a castle at Chirbury centre on the existence of an embanked platform, 58m square and up to 4.5m high, just 250m west of the village off the Chirbury–Montgomery road. It stands on a ridge with commanding views in all directions, defended by the steep fall of the valley side to its east. It may be that rare feature, a rectangular ringwork, and the fact that it lies in 'Castle Field' reinforces the belief that a royal castle stood on the site. However, excavations revealed no structural or dateable evidence and there is no other trace of a castle in Chirbury.

It is possible that the tradition derives from the Saxon foundation of a *burh* or fortress at *Cyricbyrig* by Aethelflaed in AD 915, guarding the head of the Rea–Camlad valleys, though this may have been nearer the centre of the modern village.

Chirk Bank Motte SJ 290370

A damaged mound up to 3m high stands in the grounds of Oaklands Mount at Chirk Bank. It lies 1km north of the crossroads at Weston Rhyn, above the modern canal. Sited high on a valley side, overlooking the River Ceiriog to its north, it stands directly opposite a motte on the other side of the valley at Chirk. Presumably they were intended to control the valley route on the Welsh border. The mound is approximately 35 x 25m with the remains of a ditch on its north and east sides. There is no trace of a bailey, but it may have lain to the south or west of the site, in the area now occupied by the adjacent house and gardens.

Cleobury Mortimer SO 674757

In 1066, Cleobury was granted to William Fitz Osbern but by the time of Domesday had passed to Ralph, son of Roger Mortimer. The family came from Mortemer in Normandy and gave their name to the town. Ralph was an important figure, Steward to Earl Roger, and was given a number of forfeited estates in Shropshire and Herefordshire after the unsuccessful rebellion against William I in 1074. Most were combined into the powerful Marcher lordship, the Barony of Wigmore, and remained in Mortimer hands until the execution of Roger Mortimer IV, Earl of March, in 1330. Cleobury itself was made into a Liberty in the mid-thirteenth century and absorbed most of the Mortimer estates in southern Shropshire.

It was presumably the Mortimers who built the castle which stood on high ground commanding the town centre and overlooking the road, north-west of the church of St Mary. First referred to *c.*1154, it was apparently destroyed by Henry II shortly afterwards during the rebellion of Hugh de Mortimer

41 Victorian map of Cleobury Mortimer, showing the site of the castle. All trace of it has now gone

but may have been rebuilt in the 1170s. Nothing of its structure now remains, the site largely built over, but its location is perpetuated in local names like Castle Hill. In the 1540s, Leland referred to the site 'yet called castell dike' and fragments of masonry continued to be found nearby into the eighteenth century. This implies a stone castle about which nothing is known.

It is just possible that references in the late twelfth century refer not to the castle in the town but the site at Toot Hill (q.v.).

Clun Castle so 299809 ★★★

The castle at Clun is a magnificent example of a motte and bailey, one of the finest in England, and dwarfs all the others in the county. After the Conquest, the large manor in the Forest of Clun was give to Robert (or *Picot*) de Say, whose family derived from Sai in Normandy. Robert made Clun his principal residence and under the Fitz Alans after *c.*1150 it became the centre of the

42 An aerial view of the castle at Clun. The remains of fishponds and garden features are clearly visible (bottom right). *CPAT-90-MB-948*

Barony of Clun. Apart from the castle, the Normans also laid out a planned town, to the north of the existing Saxon settlement.

The first castle would have been an earth and timber structure built by Picot de Say (d. 1098) and probably strengthened by his son Henry (d. 1130), though the first mention of it does not occur until 1146. There are further references in the Pipe Rolls of 1160-4, around which time the Honour of Clun, one of the largest estates in the county, passed by marriage to the Fitz Alans. The castle was burned by Prince Rhys ap Gruffydd after the battle of Radnor in 1195 and this damage may have led to its reconstruction in stone around 1196, with the addition of a stone keep, fragments of which remain on the east side of the motte. Clun was besieged by King John in 1216 and attacked by the Welsh who burned the town in 1234, though the castle was not taken. An inquest in 1272 on the death of John Fitz Alan refers to a tower, a grange, stables and gates but implies that much work was needed to repair or complete the buildings. The large stone keep, built into the north face of the motte, may date from the completion of the work then underway.

43 The great keep or tower block at Clun, the structure built directly into the north face of the motte

Right: 44 The castle
site at Clun

Below: 45 The massive
south bailey at Clun,
showing the very high
sides of the platform

The Fitz Alans retained ownership until 1549 but spent little time at Clun after the removal of their principal residence to Arundel in Sussex. Edward I stayed at Clun in 1295 but after the pacification of Wales the castle slowly fell into decay. Edward III may have stayed in the keep when hunting in the Forest of Clun in 1362 and around 1405, Owain Glyndwr attacked and burned the town, but is not known to have destroyed the castle. In the 1540s, Leland recorded that Clun had been 'bothe strong and well builded' but was 'somewhat ruinous'. Nevertheless, traces of fishponds and gardens around the site (especially to the west, across the river) suggest continued use as a residence after its military function had ceased. In the mid-sixteenth century Clun passed to the Howards, Dukes of Norfolk, but was forfeited to the Crown following Norfolk's part in the 1569 rebellion. Restored to the family by James I, it was sold in 1677 by Henry Howard, Earl of Northampton and repurchased by the Howard family in 1896.

The earthworks comprise two large, raised baileys, lying to the south and east of a large castle mound. The southern enclosure, approximately 75 x 35m, is defended by a ditch and bank on all but its western side and is joined by a high causeway to a smaller, rectangular eastern bailey, which is also defended by a ditch. The site is further protected by the River Clun which runs round the west and south sides of the castle. Immediately to its north, the motte is defended by a high earth bank with a deep ditch and the area beyond that was once very marshy.

The impressive motte has a summit extending to around 55 x 42m and stands to a height of nearly 11m above a ditch which is still up to 4.5m deep on the north and east sides. The summit bears fragments of a stone curtain wall and two solid semicircular towers on its western side, believed to date to the late twelfth century (*colour plate 27*). Traces of a fourteenth-century fireplace and windows reported in 1909 have since gone. On the east of the summit are the remains of a small keep, which was about 10m square.

The largest piece of masonry now remaining is the four-storey tower built into the north face of the mound. Perhaps the motte was not deemed strong enough to take the weight of such a large structure, so that its two lower floors lie below the summit of the mound, standing on a plinth with a distinct batter. The tower is believed to date from *c.*1270-80, albeit with an earlier Norman external appearance. Though it looks strong enough even in its present state, it has been regarded as a deliberately impressive domestic building – perhaps for guests' lodgings – rather than a serious fortification. Standing to a height of about 25m, the tower now measures approximately 12m wide by 21m deep, with walls 3m thick, and has square pilaster buttresses with turrets at each corner. The south face of the building has gone but would have provided the main entrance from the top of the motte. The tower contained domestic or public rooms on three floors above an unlit storeroom accessed by a stair in the west wall. The second and third floors have fireplaces in their west walls and were well lit by wide windows, which have integral stone seats. The top floor, now ruined, is believed to have been the lord's private apartment and has a fireplace in the east wall.

Although the castle was in ruins by the time of the Civil War, a Royalist garrison was stationed there, and in the town, for most of the war. Its depredations made it very unpopular with the local population, not least when the soldiers burned down the church in 1644.

Clungunford Motte so 397788 ★

The Domesday manor of *Clone* assimilated the surname of its pre-Conquest owner, Gunward, to become *Clone Gunford*. It was divided between the extensive holdings of Reginald 'the Sheriff', with most of the manor held of him by one Fulk, and with the rest lying in the Barony of Clun under Picot de Say.

46 The castle motte at Clungunford, with its centre partially dug away, giving the impression of two mounds

The mound stands on the east bank of the River Clun, possibly sited to guard a crossing. It is another Shropshire motte lying close to a church, in this case just north-east of the fourteenth-century church of St Cuthbert. The mutilated mound is fairly low (less than 4m high) and somewhat elongated. In the nineteenth century, a local vicar excavated the motte in the belief that it was a burial mound. This did serious damage and created a fissure through the centre of the mound, giving the impression of two 'peaks' to the motte. On its eastern side are traces of a ditch, which may have joined a stream to the south. There is no trace of a bailey, unless it lay in the direction of the church.

47 The small motte at Colebatch

Colebatch Motte SO 320871

The village of Colebatch was a 'member' of the large manor of Lydbury North, held in 1086 by Robert Losinga, Bishop of Hereford.

The steep-sided motte, surrounded by newly planted trees, stands in a garden near a tributary of the River Kemp, just off the present A488, 1.5km south of Bishop's Castle. The mound is over 5m high, with a summit diameter of 5m, but other than a small section visible as a slight depression on the south-west side, there is no trace of the surrounding ditch nor is there any sign of a bailey.

Colstey Motte SO 303841

A mound is said to have stood near 'Castle Field' at Colstey, south of Argoed. It was destroyed between 1966-73 but may have been a motte controlling the old road through a steep-sided valley. Nothing now remains and nothing is known of its history. The site at Acton Bank (q.v.) is only 1.5km to the north-east along the same route.

Corfham Castle SO 525850 ★★

The large manor of Corfham was the centre or *caput* of the Hundred of Culverstone in 1086 and was in royal ownership before the Conquest. Along with other royal manors, it was held directly by Earl Roger until the confiscation of the family's estates in 1102. It remained for the most part in royal hands until granted to the Clifford family by Henry II.

The original castle may have been built by Walter de Clifford (d.1190), father of Henry II's famous mistress, 'the fair Rosamund', but the first

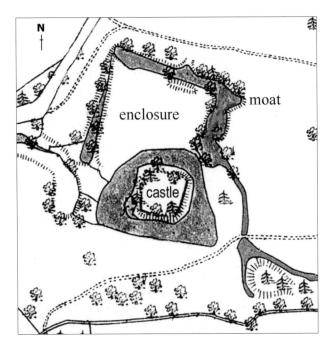

48 Plan of the site of Corfham castle, showing its extensive water features and defences

49 The main castle platform at Corfham, looking across its moat from the north

reference to it occurs in 1232 when it was confiscated from Walter de Clifford III following his rebellion against Henry III. The castle passed to the Giffards in 1271 but was recorded as ruinous on the death of John Giffard in 1299. It must have been repaired when it came into the hands of Fulk le Strange early in the fourteenth century and there are references to it into the 1380s. The castle was again in ruins by the mid-sixteenth century.

Corfham is an interesting site, surrounded by the remains of banks and moats. It lies some 600m west of the village of Peaton, at the northern edge of a low ridge between the River Corve to the west and the Pye Brook to the east. Water for its moats was originally diverted from the Pye Brook and discharged into the Corve from the western arm of the outer moat. Surrounded by its water-filled moats, Corfham would have been an imposing sight in its heyday in the mid-fourteenth century.

The actual castle stood on a roughly rectangular raised platform 30 x 40m at its summit and about 2m above the level of its moat. Low mounds around the perimeter of this platform mark the location of stone towers (at each corner) and connecting walls. The platform is surrounded by an inner moat which is up to 15m wide; its low-lying ground is still boggy in wet weather.

North of the inner moat is a well-defined rectangular enclosure, 70 x 50m, surrounded by the remains of substantial banks and ditches. These are most clearly visible to the north where the rampart is up to 7m wide and nearly 2m high. The whole enclosure, except on the southern side facing the castle, is protected by its own moat which at its south-eastern branch (where the water supply entered the system) widens to encompass a mound which may have had something to do with water regulation.

Fragments of the castle's masonry – presumably part of the towers, a rectangular hall, gateway defences or curtain walls – were still standing in the late nineteenth century, but nothing remains visible today apart from scattered pieces of stone lying about the site.

Corfton Motte SO 497846 ★

In 1086 the manor of Corfton was held of Earl Roger by Roger de Lacy, with Herbert as his subtenant. A sizeable motte and bailey castle known as 'The Mount' lies on the north-east end of a low ridge overlooking the Corve valley. It is immediately adjacent to Hill House Farm, some of whose buildings (which include a medieval chapel) encroach onto the site.

The large oval motte is 5-6m high, measuring approximately 37 x 25m at its summit with an earthwork 'parapet' around its rim, highest on the southern side. The motte is surrounded by a ditch, with a distinct outer bank rising to over 1m high on its southern section. On sloping ground east of the motte lies a roughly rectangular bailey, 120 x 100m, divided into two enclosures by a low bank. The perimeter defences of the bailey – the usual ditch and bank – are still discernible for most of their length. The best-preserved section is the ditch around the southern length of the bailey, where it is approximately

50 The castle mound at Corfton. The encroachment of farm buildings can be seen on the left

7m wide and up to 1.5m deep. A sunken lane at the east of the bailey may follow the perimeter ditch in that area.

Cressage Motte SJ 592042

Before and just after the Conquest, *Christesache* ('Christ's Oak') was held by Edric 'the Wild', a leading Saxon nobleman with extensive Shropshire estates. Though he retained his lands after the Conquest, he became involved in a series of uprisings against William in 1067, in 1069 and perhaps in 1075. Not surprisingly, he had lost his estates by 1086. Cressage was then held from Earl Roger by Ranulf as one of four manors held by him in Condover hundred. The manor reverted to the Crown under Henry I *c.*1130 and subsequently passed through various families – the de Lacys by 1180, the Baskervilles in the mid-fourteenth century and their relatives the Foulhursts by 1383.

Ranulf Peverel or his son William built the original castle at Cressage. It stood at the foot of Cressage Hill, in what is now the angle between the B4380 and the Cressage–Sheinton road and may have controlled a crossing of the Severn.

Little now survives of the motte, which was largely destroyed by the construction of the Severn Valley Railway, 1860–62, which cut through it. A fragment remains in the grounds of The Old Hall and indicates a motte approximately 4m high. The bailey extended southwards, away from the river, into the area between the two modern roads. Its outline is reflected in the alignment of local gardens and in the ground levels in the area, and a small section of its ditch survives as an ornamental pond in the Hall gardens.

A manor house is recorded in the bailey as early as *c.*1369, by which time one supposes that the 'defensive' nature of the site had lost its significance, the castle mound had been abandoned and the bailey adapted to purely domestic use. The present Old Hall is the successor to the original manor house and was constructed *c.*1670.

Culmington Motte and Bailey SO 497821 ★★

In fields approximately 300m north-east of the late Saxon church of All Saints in Culmington, is a well-preserved early medieval site. It is dominated

51 Aerial photo of the impressive site at Culmington, clearly showing its associated enclosures and clear marks of ridge-and-furrow features. *CPAT-89-MB-68*

by the motte and bailey castle of 'Camp Ring' with its associated enclosures and field systems. Earl Roger himself held the manor in 1086 and gave part of the its tithes to his new church at Quatford (q.v.); it later became part of the manor of Corfham.

The motte lies on a low ridge above former water meadows flooded by the Pye Brook to its east and another stream to its south (*colour plate 22*). The motte is now quite low, just over 2m high and 27m in diameter. The surrounding ditch is up to 8m wide and 1m deep, and is water-filled on its eastern side. Its bailey extends to the south-west of the motte, with a wide enclosing ditch and bank, crossed by a causeway on its south-west side. In the fields to the east and south of the motte are two further well-defined enclosures, with their own ditch and bank perimeters, now largely ploughed away. It is likely that these were associated with the castle or were linked to agricultural usage and with the field systems surrounding the site.

Dawley Castle SJ 687063

By the time of Domesday, Dawley Magna had separated from the manor of Wellington and was held by William Pandolf or Pantulf of the family of the barons of Wem. The earliest reference to a castle at *Dailileye*, which stood some 250m south-east of the church of Holy Trinity at Dawley Magna, is a patent of 1316 allowing Walter de Morton (or Mouton) to fortify his mansion there. It passed soon afterwards to the Fitz Alan family. The castle may have been abandoned by the mid-fifteenth century, but the manor had descended through various families by the seventeenth century and the castle may have been restored, or a new house constructed on or near the site.

Dawley was garrisoned for the King in 1643 but contemporary news-sheets imply that it changed hands, being in Parliamentary occupation by October 1643, but with a Royalist garrison in May 1645. It seems to have been abandoned in the summer of 1645 when its Royalist garrison set fire to it. The castle was briefly involved in the renewed Civil War in 1648 when an unsuccessful attempt to seize it on behalf of the King was made by Sir Henry Lingen. As a result Parliament ordered its demolition July 1648.

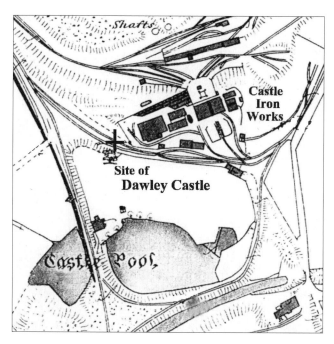

52 Victorian plan of the site of Dawley Castle. Nothing now remains visible

By *c*.1760, the castle was used as a farmstead whose buildings and part of the moat survived into the nineteenth century. However, industrial development in the area destroyed what remained and the site was buried beneath the slagheaps of the adjacent Castle Furnaces, which operated between 1810 and 1883. The surviving 'Castle Pool' is now thought to relate to the industrial process rather than to the original castle, of which nothing now remains.

East Dudston Farm Motte so 245974

The manor of Dudston was one of the holdings of Earl Roger and formed part of the Honour of Montgomery. It eventually came into the hands of the Fitz Herbert family.

The motte at Dudston lies off the B4386 Montgomery–Chirbury road, in the grounds of East Dudston Farm. It has been badly damaged by farm building, which has eaten into its northern and north-eastern sides, removing over half of the structure. What remains is a tree-covered fragment, 4m high and 13m across the summit. The ditch has been more or less filled in, though it is discernible on the south side. The location of the bailey is not known.

53 The fragmentary remains of the castle mound at East Dudston farm

54 The mound – a tumulus or a motte – at Eaton near Bishop's Castle

Eaton Mound SO 374895

In the gardens of a farm at Eaton, on the A489 near Bishop's Castle, are the remains of a man-made mound, the origin of which is disputed. It overlooks the valley of the Onny to its north and east. The mound, whose original diameter was about 18m, was damaged by road widening in 1856 so that only half remains, standing to a height of about 3m. When dug into, fragments of burned pottery and human remains were found, as reported in the *Illustrated London News* of October 1856. This has led to suggestions that the feature is a burial mound rather than a motte. If it was a motte – or a barrow re-used as one – there is no trace of a surrounding ditch or bailey, though the latter may have lain in the area of the present farm.

Ellesmere Castle SJ 404346 ★★

Ellesmere was one of the personal holdings of Earl Roger in 1086 and its castle may have been built by the Earl himself around 1070. Passing into royal hands, it was granted by Henry I to the Peverel family and is referred to in 1138 by Orderic Vitalis. But because of its strategic location on the Welsh

73

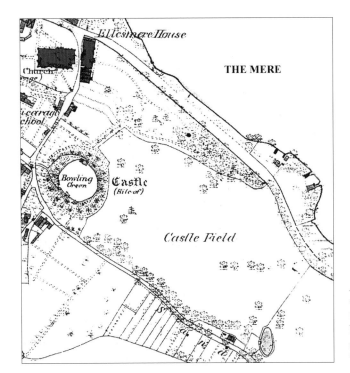

55 The site of Ellesmere Castle. The bailey lay in the area marked 'Castle Field'

56 Banks and ditches defending the bailey at Ellesmere. The motte lies in the trees to the right of the photograph

frontier, it has a complicated history of ownership, passing for long periods (e.g. 1177-1208) into the hands of Welsh princes. It appears to have been reconstructed by 1241, following destruction (in a Welsh attack of 1208) and subsequent abandonment. There are references to building work and repairs in royal accounts throughout the thirteenth century, even though the castle had passed to the le Strange family in 1267. Further repairs are recorded in 1309 but it seems to have been abandoned by *c.*1330 and Leland could only refer to the *site* of the castle at the time of his visit. Although this important town on the Chester–Shrewsbury route was frequently caught up in the Civil War, there is no reference to any activity at the castle, which presumably had been long abandoned.

The motte and bailey stands on a ridge to the south-east of the town, approx 100m from the medieval church of St Mary. The large mound was shaped from a glacial bank and provided a commanding height with outstanding views to its south and over the town and mere (*colour plate 28*). The steep-sided motte is very impressive, though its impact is reduced nowadays because it is shrouded in trees and undergrowth. Standing to over 11m high it has a levelled summit, 50m in diameter, now used as a bowling green. There is no trace of stonework or masonry on the site. Its surrounding ditch is very deep and wide, especially on its southern side, and extends in places to a width of 20m and a depth of over 3m. The roughly quadrangular bailey to the south is rather small but may have been reduced by quarrying and much of its south-eastern section has gone. The bailey has a massive outer bank and ditch, the former up to 13m wide and 2m high and the latter up to 15m wide and 1m deep, which would have provided a formidable defensive barrier.

Earthworks to the north and north-west of the motte (embracing the site of the church) may be traces of another bailey associated with the castle, though they could be more modern, the result of later building and landscaping. The present Sandy Lane may follow the line of a former defensive ditch.

Fitz Motte SJ 448178

The Domesday manor of *Witesot* (later corrupted to *Fitz*) was held by Picot de Say and descended with the Fitz Alans, lords of Clun. What is left of the circular motte lies on a farm near the Norman church of St Peter and St Paul, but only a fragment remains; much of its north-eastern half was removed by farm building

57 The remains of the motte at Fitz. The church of St Peter and St Paul is visible to the right

by 1901, when burnt layers and bone fragments were found. It then had diameters of 30m and 16m at base and summit respectively and was about 4m high.

Ford Hall Farm Ringwork SJ 651326

The most recent discovery of a previously unrecorded castle is that on the aptly-named 'Castle Hill', 500m south-east of Ford Hall farm and 1.5km south-west of Little Drayton. Forestry clearance in 1975 revealed a D-shaped ringwork formed from a glacial mound, occupying a strong defensive position above a loop in the River Tern. Its bailey lay to the north-west, separated from the ringwork by a wide ditch. The ringwork has a base diameter of about 65m, an internal diameter of approximately 35m, with the interior some 3m above the outside ground level. Its summit is enclosed by a substantial rampart up to 2m high, with an entrance on the south-west side.

It has been suggested that the site may be the castle of *Moretoin* mentioned in 1215 (but see also More, below) or the site of a castle noted by Leland as *Draiton apon Terne*.

Gobowen Motte SJ 303340

The slight remains of a low motte stand in the field of Bryn-y-Castell ('Castle Hill'), along the B5069 in Gobowen. It is immediately west of Preeshenlle United Reformed Chapel, whose construction in the mid-nineteenth century ate into the side of the mound. Sited on the northern slope of a natural spur overlooking the flood plain of the Perry, it has good views to the north and east. The castle lay on the western side of Wat's Dyke, but since all trace of this has been lost in the area, it is impossible to establish the relationship between the motte and the earlier earthwork. The castle may have incorporated part of Wat's Dyke within its own perimeters. Nothing is known of its history.

58 The low remains of the motte at Bryn-y-Castell, Gobowen, with the chapel to the right

Hagley Mound SO 278975

It has been suggested that a mound near an orchard at Hagley, surrounded by early ridge and furrow features, may be a castle motte. Nothing is known of its history and some consider it to be just a natural feature.

59 The overgrown castle mound at Hardwicke. The farm lies to the left of this photograph

Hardwick Motte SO 368906 ★

Hardwick (or Hardwicke) was part of the manor of Lydbury North, but the builder of the sizeable motte there is unknown. It is close to a modern mill pond near Hardwick Farm, part of which directly abuts the south-east side of the site. The mound stands on the slope of a ridge near the East Onny river and was presumably intended to control the southern end of the valley route between the Long Mynd and the Stiperstones.

The circular motte, now overgrown, stands to a height of 3m, its flat summit having a diameter of approximately 15m. There is a trace of a surrounding ditch and bank, most clearly visible around the north-west side but the site of its bailey is not known. It is assumed to have lain to the north-west of the motte, its perimeter perhaps represented by a curving earthwork bank, but with no visible trace of an outer ditch.

Harley Motte SJ 596012

It has been speculated that 'Castle Hill' in Harley is the site of a motte relating to John de Harley, who accompanied the First Crusade in 1098. However, there is no documentary proof that a castle existed on the site and some consider it to be a natural feature.

Hawcocks Farm Ringwork SJ 349078 ★★

The interesting ringwork of Hawcock's Mount stands on the old Westbury–Montgomery road, near the vanished village of Winsley. At the time of Domesday, this was held by Roger Corbet but was eventually 'deserted', and is now represented only by Hawcock's Farm and the nearby Winsley Hall. It is assumed that Hawcock's Mount was the predecessor of Caus (q.v.) just over 1km to the west, since the name is said to be a corruption of *Aldecause* ('Old Cause'), a name which occurs as early as 1381. Whilst the site is lower in the Rea Brook valley than Caus and would have allowed more immediate access to the Shrewsbury–Montgomery route, it does not have the commanding views afforded by Caus. It is possible that Hawcocks remained in use for some time alongside Caus as an outpost.

60 Part of the ringwork at Hawcocke's Mount showing what may have been the original entrance at its north-eastern side

61 Part of the mound and surrounding ditch at Hawcocke's

The castle was built by the Corbets, possibly by William Corbet in the 1070s. His successor, Roger, forfeited his estates to Henry I following his involvement in Robert de Bellême's rebellion in 1102. They were restored to the family *c.*1115 and it may have been around that time that Roger adopted Caus as his principal seat. Between 1121-35, the Corbets gave Winsley to Shrewsbury Abbey, the date perhaps linked with the transference of their seat to Caus whose castle is first mentioned in 1140.

Hawcock's Mount stands on an east-facing slope above the Rea Brook valley and is a fine example of a ringwork. It has a summit diameter of approximately 35m with a wide earth rampart standing up to 1.5m around its perimeter. The steeply-sided central mound rises 6-7m above its surrounding ditch, which is up to 2m deep and 7m wide. This is most clearly defined around the west and south sides of the motte and is still water-filled in places. A causeway and entrance, possibly modern, passes through the south-west of the site. The remains have been damaged by quarrying on the north-eastern side, close to what may be the original entrance, which crosses the ditch and cuts through the rampart.

Heath Farm Ringwork SJ 379113

The ringwork which lies close to Heath Farm is all that remains of the ancient settlement of Amaston. The manor was another held of Earl Roger in 1086 by Almund and his son Alward and became part of the Honour of Montgomery. It had seven tenants in 1086 but only four by 1379 – perhaps reflecting the impact of the Black Death. The hamlet survived into the late seventeenth century but gradually died out leaving only the present farm of *c*.1800, now called Heath Farm but once known as Amaston Farm.

The remains are very eroded. The ringwork itself rises on average only 2m above the surrounding land, encircled by a shallow ditch, and is approximately

62 Aerial view of the castle at Heath Farm, Amaston, with the low motte to the left and the bailey to the right. The site is bisected by the farm road. *CPAT-85-9-13*

32m across. Its bailey lies across the farm road to the north-west, just visible as a low platform about 1m high and extending to approximately 45 x 40m.

Hisland Motte SJ 317275

Hideslond stands on the medieval frontier with Wales, just east of Wat's Dyke, and has a complicated history of ownership. It was once part of the Honour of Montgomery, but for much of its early history lay outside the Shropshire border in Wales and was held for a time by Haughmond Abbey.

Nothing is known of the history of the motte at Hisland. It stands in the grounds of a farm whose buildings may occupy the bailey site, which is otherwise unidentified. The steep-sided earth and rubble mound, now very overgrown, is roughly oval and rises to approximately 4m high. It stands on the eastern slope of a natural spur with good views in all directions, especially to the south. Shallow traces of its surrounding ditch survive only to the north and west of the motte.

63 The overgrown motte at Hisland. The modern farm lies to the left rear of this photograph

Hockleton Motte and Bailey SO 274999 *

Hockleton, north of Chirbury, was part of the Honour of Montgomery, linked to Earl Roger's new castle there. The manor was held of the Earl by the de Hockleton family, who owed service to the castle at Montgomery, and it may have been William de Hockleton who built the motte and bailey in the late eleventh century.

The castle, an attractive example of the type dotted along the Rea–Camlad valleys, occupies the end of a ridge south of the present Hockleton bridge. It is close to (but not actually on) the edge of the river bank above a narrow gorge on the Camlad and probably controlled a river crossing. The castle may reflect not only an attempt by the new Norman lords to control an important route but also the deliberate settlement of the area.

Hockleton can never have been very significant. Its small conical motte stands to a height of approximately 3.5m above its bailey, with a summit of only 6m diameter and probably supported little more than a watchtower. Traces of its wide surrounding ditch now remain visible only to the south.

64 Aerial view of the small motte and bailey at Hockleton. *CPAT*

Fanning out to the north of the motte, which forms its southern side, the bailey is a clearly-defined raised platform, 2m high and extending to approximately 38 x 30m. There is no clear trace of a surrounding ditch, but the bailey entrance lay to the north, where a gap is still visible (*colour plate 6*).

Hodnet Motte and Bailey SJ 614284 ★

'Castle Hill' within the grounds of Hodnet Hall is a fine example of a small motte and bailey. The motte, now obscured by trees and undergrowth, lies on a south-facing slope some 200m south-east of the Saxon church of St Luke. After the conquest, the manor of Hodnet, a royal holding under Edward the Confessor, became part of the personal estates of Earl Roger, who granted the church to Shrewsbury Abbey. It passed to the Honour of Montgomery under Baldwin de Boulers after the rebellion of Robert of Bellême and the confiscation of his estates. Held by the de Hodnet family as tenants, it was probably Baldwin de Hodnet who built the castle late in the eleventh century, though the earliest reference to it is as late as 1223. The manor later passed to the Vernon and de Ludlow families.

The flat-topped motte has steep sides and stands 6-7m high, surrounded by an impressive ditch partly cut through rock, up to 3m deep and 8m wide. Excavations in the late nineteenth century revealed traces of stone buildings and, on its western side, the remains of a strong circular or octagonal keep constructed in red sandstone which may have been destroyed by fire. The mound, whose summit extends to 25 x 30m lies at the south-east corner of a rectangular 'inner bailey', some 100 x 60m, whose northern section has been destroyed by later landscaping. To its west, separated from it by a deep ditch 10m wide, is another, triangular enclosure or 'outer bailey', part of whose perimeter ditch and bank is clearly visible, especially on its western side.

Holdgate Castle SO 562897 ★★

Holdgate manor, originally known as Stanton, was one of 17 in Shropshire held of Earl Roger by Helgot, one of the Earl's leading tenants, from whom it later took its name. His lands formed the Barony of Castle Holdgate. Helgot built the original castle, one of only three in Shropshire (with

Above: 65 Part of the overgrown motte at Hodnet

Right: 66 Plan *c.*1880 of the site at Hodnet, the motte to the lower right and the traces of its baileys to the left

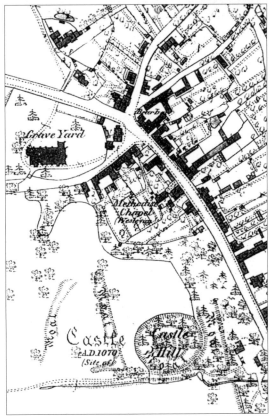

67 The farmhouse at Holdgate, incorporating the round tower of the thirteenth-century stone castle

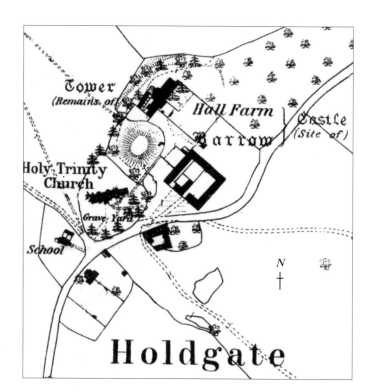

68 Late Victorian plan of the site at Holdgate

69 The large motte at Holdgate which originally bore a stone tower

Shrewsbury and Oswestry) mentioned in Domesday Book. Further references occur in 1109 (when Henry I was entertained there by Herbert Fitz Helgot), in 1216 and in 1281. Under Henry III, a charter was granted for a weekly fair at Holdgate and the whole settlement, with its fine church, its large motte and the thirteenth-century tower, is of great historical interest.

The castle occupies the northern end of a low ridge to the east of Corve Dale and is adjacent to the church of The Holy Trinity. Like the castle, the church and its priest are recorded in Domesday Book, though the church was rebuilt *c*.1115-9. Interestingly, references to the new church state that it lay within the castle defences and it is assumed that the present churchyard lies within the first bailey associated with the motte. The manor passed to the Maudit family in 1204 and then through various hands, including those of the Knights Templar. By 1210 a college of secular clergy was established within the precincts of the castle; it was dissolved *c*.1373. The castle was apparently a ruin when purchased in 1284 by Bishop Burnell (see Acton Burnell) and he may have built the fine stone tower which survives. However, at the time of Burnell's death in 1292, the castle was described as having no value. Holdgate descended in the Burnell family until granted by Henry VIII to the Howards, Dukes of Norfolk, and from them to other families.

Although shrouded in trees, the steep, oval motte is an impressive feature, standing to a height of 8-10m. It extends to 50 x 45m at its base and 18 x 12m at its summit. Stone fragments on the flat summit are the remains of the foundations of a tower, perhaps built by the Maudits. An ice-house was later built into the mound. Part of the substantial ditch surrounding the motte is visible around its south-west and west sides, extending to 11m wide and 2m deep in places. This separates the motte from the churchyard to its south-west but later building work and roadways have removed any traces of the ditch in other areas.

There were two baileys associated with the motte. To its south-west lies a smaller, probably earlier, enclosure. The platform is a rounded triangle with internal dimensions of 77 x 65m, defined by a steep scarp up to 2m high. It now forms the churchyard of the church of The Holy Trinity, which lies in the middle of the enclosure, conforming to early references to the church being within the perimeters of the castle.

A larger, and probably later, bailey extended to the north-east of the motte in the area now occupied by Hall Farm. Although most of its earthwork perimeters have been lost to later building, enough remains to indicate that the platform was roughly rectangular with internal dimensions of 130 x 60m. The perimeter is defined by a scarp some 70m long and nearly 1m high, running from the north of the motte, curving to the east and marking the north-west corner of the bailey. It continues along the north side for 50m before turning south and fading away. The north-west section of this scarp merges into the hillside, sloping gently to the west. The east side of the platform is no longer visible, having been levelled by later building. However the scarp is visible around the south-eastern side, falling to the road below. This bailey was probably surrounded by a stone curtain wall and its masonry and stonework from the castle was no doubt re-used in the construction of the later farmhouse and buildings. To the south-east of the motte and bailey a series of rectangular enclosures may represent the remains of formal gardens associated with later phases of the castle.

Built into a later farmhouse in the north-west quarter of the bailey is a two-storey, semicircular mural tower of fine ashlar, believed to be late thirteenth century in date, all that survives of the stone castle. It is approximately 8m in diameter with walls 10m high and has narrow slit windows and a modern conical, tiled roof.

What little evidence there is suggests that Holdgate, then owned by the Cressett family, was held by a Royalist garrison as an outpost of Ludlow during the Civil War. With Parliamentary forces pushing southwards after the fall of Shrewsbury in February 1645, it seems that its garrison slighted the castle and withdrew. A contemporary Parliamentary report claimed that it was too ruinous to refortify and was simply abandoned.

Hope Motte SJ 344023 ★

In 1086, Hope was one of the outliers of the large manor of Worthen, part of the demesne land of the Corbets. The motte stands south-west of Lady House Farm on a ridge whose ground falls away to the north and overlooks the valley of the Rea Brook. It commands good views in all directions.

The tree-capped mound, clearly visible on the skyline when seen from the south, is a good example of a small motte. It rises to a height of about 3m, with a base diameter of 23m and a summit diameter of 8-9m. Shallow traces of its ditch, up to 3m wide, survive on all but the east side but there is no trace of a bailey, which may have lain the direction of the modern farm.

70 The motte near Lady House Farm at Hope

Hopton Castle SO 367779 ★★

At the time of Domesday, Hopton was one of the extensive holdings of Robert (*Picot*) de Say (d.1098), one of Earl Roger's foremost tenants, and formed part of the Barony of Clun. The barony passed by marriage to the Fitz Alans in the late twelfth century and joined their Barony of Oswestry. The manor's tenants from 1165 were the de Hopton family, with service at Clun castle as part of their tenurial obligation. A reference in 1264 to the seizure of cattle by Walter de Hopton, who took them to his 'castles' at Hopton, may indicate that the nearby ringwork at Warfield Bank (q.v.) was also occupied at that time. Hopton passed to the Corbets in the mid-fifteenth century, the village being known for a time as Hopton Corbet. It was sold to the Wallop family in the early sixteenth century and was held by them at the time of the Civil War.

Hopton Castle is one of comparatively few in Shropshire for which information on its Civil War activities survives in some detail. Owned by the anti-Royalist Henry Wallop, it was held in 1644 by a Parliamentary garrison of 31 men under Capt. Samuel More. In February 1644 it was besieged by a Royalist force from Ludlow under Sir Michael Woodhouse which suffered

71 The keep at Hopton, standing on the remains of the original motte

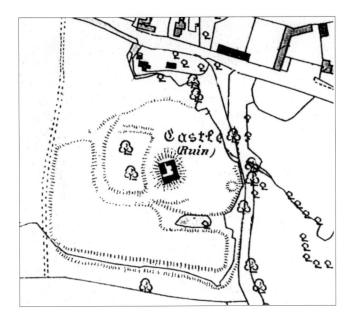

72 Plan of the castle site at Hopton

severe casualties in various assaults. However, after a fortnight's siege, the inner bailey was breached and the porch to the keep was burned. After this attack, the garrison agreed to surrender on what they thought would be honourable terms, but were then 'cruelly and treacherously put to death' by (depending on which version of the story one accepts) being beaten and buried alive in the moat or shot and buried in the moat. Only two of the defenders escaped. The massacre was regarded as retribution for the deaths of up to 200 Royalist soldiers killed in the siege. The castle was slighted immediately afterwards and although it is may have been repaired to some extent, it was a ruin by 1731.

The site displays an interesting arrangement of mounds and ditches representing not only perimeter defences but a fishpond and water management features. The castle occupies a low-lying, marshy area bounded on three sides by streams which originally supplied its water defences. The mound on which the keep stands is the remnant of the original motte. It is about 2m high, with a base diameter of 32m, and retains traces of its surrounding ditch. There is a well-defined bailey, defended by a wide ditch, to the north, west and east of the keep, with a large building platform on its western side. This inner bailey appears to have been defended by a weak stone curtain wall (breached in 1644) with square towers at the corners. A large L-shaped outer bailey, which may have been a later addition extending the defences on that side, lies to the south and west of the keep and has equally well-defined boundaries in the form of a low bank and a ditch which is up to 12m wide in places.

The date of the construction of the first stone castle is unclear – perhaps as early as 1231 (when Henry II may have stayed) or later in the century under Sir Walter de Hopton (d.1305). Fragments of square towers found at the corners of the inner bailey may relate to his tenure.

The main structure, an impressive rectangular keep, is believed to date to the very late thirteenth or early fourteenth century. Like Clun and Wattlesborough (q.v.) its form is anachronistic, resembling earlier types of Norman keep – perhaps reflecting the conservatism of a remote area where old forms continued in favour. The three-storey rubble and sandstone tower stands on a battered plinth and has buttresses reinforcing its corners. It measures approximately 14 x 13m with walls over 3m thick at their base, becoming thinner as they rise. The main entrance is on the north side and shows traces of the porch burned in 1644. A smaller doorway in the west wall led, via a causeway (and possible drawbridge across the ditch) to the domestic buildings in the bailey. In the late sixteenth century, a small attic room was added below the gabled roof, which presumably had a battlemented parapet. Apart from the usual stairwells and latrines, the tower housed two large living rooms, the fireplaces of which are still visible in the north face. The lower storey has a central room with deep window recesses giving access to four small chambers set into the corners of the building. The upper chamber is larger and more open, with double-light windows and small rectangular rooms – perhaps bedchambers – set into the walls.

South of Hopton Castle, 700m north of Bedstone church, is an earthwork known as Rabbit Berries (SO 367765). It is regarded as an eroded burial mound, shaped from the side of a knoll, but may be the remains of a motte.

Kinton Motte SJ 370194

Kinton was a 'member' of the manor of Ness, originally one of Earl Roger's own holdings. On the forfeiture of Robert of Bellême's estates in 1102, it reverted to the king and was granted by Henry II to the le Strange family *c*.1157.

73 Little now remains of the motte in the gardens of Castle Cottages at Kinton apart from this barely discernible slope (rear right)

The slight remains of a motte lie in the gardens of the aptly-named 'Castle Cottages' in Kinton. It stood on a ridge running north-west to south-east, allowing commanding views over the surrounding land, especially to its south. The mound is hardly distinguishable in the gardens other than as a slight slope to the south, and its south-eastern side has been cut away by the road. There is no trace of a bailey, though the sunken lane running around the south-west of the site may represent part of the original ditch separating the motte from the bailey. This may have lain to the west, in an area now occupied by gardens and houses.

Knockin Castle SJ 336224 ★

Knockin has no entry in Domesday Book and is believed to be a 'planned settlement' of the mid-twelfth century, carved out of the Saxon manor of Osbaston. In 1086, Osbaston was held of Earl Roger by the Fitz Alan family and from them as tenants by the le Stranges. The castle is thought to have been constructed *c*.1150-60 by Guy le Strange and repairs are recorded in 1165 and 1198 when it was briefly in royal hands. Its stone defences, of which only an overgrown fragment remains on the south of the site, may have been built in the 1220s. The castle was occupied by the le Strange family up to the death of Maude le Strange in 1405, ultimately passing to the Stanleys, Earls of Derby, *c*.1482. It was already in ruins when visited by Leland and its stone-work was gradually robbed to build other features in the village, such as the church wall and bridge.

The motte and bailey, lying in the Rectory grounds, is very impressive, though now obscured by trees. The motte is a large oblong 45 x 50m at its summit and up to 7m high, standing in a roughly quadrangular raised inner bailey approximately 56 x 40m. The bailey's high bank and ditch encircle the south and west sides of the mound but any defences to the east – now the Rectory garden – have vanished. There are fragments of masonry, perhaps from the stone curtain wall of the inner bailey and including the top of a buried archway, on the south-eastern side of the site. A watercolour *c*.1840 shows two fairly complete gateway towers still in situ.

It is has been suggested that an outer bailey lay to the east of the castle, where the present Rectory and its gardens lie, but there must have been another to the west, where the church of St Mary stands. Built by Ralph le

74 Part of the north bank of the castle mound at Knockin

75 Part of the bailey (south side) at Knockin. As can be seen, the entire site is obscured by trees and undergrowth

Strange and consecrated in 1190, the church is only a few metres from the bank on that side and must have lain within the castle's perimeter. However, modern building on this side has destroyed any surface remains. The site is framed to the west (between the motte and the church) and to the east by two streams ultimately deriving from one source 0.5km to the north. These may have been diverted around the castle to augment its defences; the eastern side was certainly marshy and flooded periodically within living memory.

Lea Castle so 351892

Lea is one of few examples in Shropshire of a castle that survived as an integral part of a later building, in this case a Victorian farmhouse. Wattlesborough and Holdgate are others. Lea was part of the manor of Lydbury North, held by the Bishops of Hereford, and an earlier castle may have been built here by the bishop. However, what remains is thought to have been constructed by the Corbets in the early fourteenth century; Robert Corbet is recorded as residing here in the 1320s after Lydbury North manor was confiscated by Edward II. The castle remained in Corbet hands until the Civil War.

During the war, Lea held a Royalist garrison as an outpost of Bishop's Castle, though for how long is not known. On 18 October 1645, a news-sheet reported that Sir Thomas Middleton 'hath performed much gallant service, and in particular he sent forth a party of foot to Leigh about a mile from Bishop's Castle, where the enemy had left a garrison, which fled away before his forces came near them'. The castle is reported to have been demolished by order of Parliament.

Little remains apart from the crumbling, ivy-clad ruins of one square tower (approximately 5 x 14m), lacking its northern wall, built into the north side of a farmhouse. The stonework is Wenlock limestone with ashlar dressings and stands to a maximum height of just over 5m, with walls approximately 2m thick. Features reported in late Victorian accounts – other windows, part of a staircase and a portcullis – no longer exist.

The extent of the original castle is not clear, but traces of possible moats exist nearby and on what looks like a raised platform in the orchard west of the house are earth banks which could be associated with the castle defences. The whole site is badly decayed and in danger of further loss.

76 A sketch of the ruins at Lea *c.*1891, when rather more of the structure still remained

Left: 77 The only surviving fragment of the stone castle at Lea, which was incorporated into the back of a Victorian farmhouse

Below: 78 The large mound at Castle Farm, Leebotwood

Leebotwood Mound SO 446991

At Castle Hill Farm, 400m north of the church of St Mary at Leebotwood, stands a distinctive mound. However, although it resembles a fairly large motte its origins are unclear. The hillock slopes gently from north to south and extends to approximately 75m long and 50m across. It stands to a height of 5m and is bounded on its south and east sides by streams. The mound has been described as the site of a medieval house, as a burial mound, as a motte or simply as a natural feature. The consensus seems to be that 'Castle Hill' is a glacial mound, with nothing pointing to its use as a house or castle.

Lee Brockhurst Mound SJ 546272

The manor of Lee Brockhurst was held in 1086 by Norman *Venator* 'the Hunter'. He and his brother Roger were huntsmen to Earl Roger and were granted manors near Shropshire's forest areas. Roger was the founder of the de Pitchford family, in whose hands the manor of Lee Brockhurst and his other holdings descended.

Nothing remains of a motte, said to have been 3m high, which reportedly stood north-east of the church at Lee Brockhurst. The site was levelled *c.*1962 and has been built over.

Little Ness Motte SJ 407197 ★

In 1086 Little Ness was one of the extensive holdings of Reginald (Reinald) de Bailleul, Sheriff of Shropshire under his kinsman Earl Roger. After the rebellion of 1102, it passed into the Fitz Alan barony of Oswestry.

The small conical motte is 5-6m high, with steeply sloping sides but with only the faintest remnant of a surrounding ditch. Less than 50m to its north-west lies the twelfth-century church of St Martins and its churchyard. These occupy what was the raised bailey associated with the motte, the churchyard wall possibly defining its boundary. No traces of ditches or other perimeter earthworks are visible in the fields nearby.

79 The small conical motte at Little Ness

80 Little Shrawardine: the base of the motte and part of its surrounding ditch. The ditch here became part of a trackway leading from the village to a ferry point on the Severn

Little Shrawardine Motte and Bailey sj 393151 ★

Little Shrawardine was a sizeable village in the Middle Ages – one of many in Shropshire which have shrunk or vanished altogether. At the time of Domesday, it was an 'outlier' of the manor of Ford, held by Earl Roger but after the forfeiture of the family's Shropshire estates in 1102, the manor remained in royal hands for much of the twelfth century. Around 1230 it passed to the Audleys, who held it into the fifteenth century, but today Little Shrawardine Farm and its castle is all that remains of the ancient village.

It is not known who built the impressive motte overlooking the Severn, though a castle existed by 1165 when repairs are recorded. At that time, the manor of Ford was briefly held by the Earl of Cornwall. The castle is known to have been rebuilt *c*.1220. There was a river crossing here (linked to Shrawardine (q.v.) on the opposite bank) and for generations a ferry point. Both castles would have controlled the valley, the river route and its crossings. It has been suggested that Little Shrawardine was the predecessor of the larger Alberbury (q.v.), which became the *caput* of the Hundred of Ford.

The remains comprise a substantial motte, now largely obscured by trees, standing up to 9m from ground level and towering above the Severn to over 15m on the river side. Although part of north-western (river) face of the mound has been washed away, from across the river it is an imposing sight. The summit bears fragments of what may have been a square stone keep, believed to date to the late twelfth century. A quadrangular bailey about 70 x 60m lies to its north-east, defended on its north-west side by the steep slope falling to the river. Slight traces of a defensive bank remain on its south and south-west sides. The deep ditch between the motte and the bailey was long used as a trackway from the village to the crossing point on the Severn, dominated by the castle. The castle ditch and surrounding bank, which have been washed away by the river to the west, continue to be visible around the motte to the south-west.

Lower Down Motte SO 336846 ★★

Little is known about the interesting site near Lower Down Farm. The motte lies on the summit of a rounded hill whose ground falls away to the north and affords excellent views in that direction. The mound has a base diameter of approximately 35m, a summit diameter of 18m and stands to a height of over

81 The motte at Lower Down with its impressive surrounding ditch

4.5m. The centre and eastern sides have been dug out, presumably to rob the foundations of a shell keep which stood on the summit. What may have been a section of its wall was visible into modern times on the south-west side of the motte and other substantial stone foundations have been found. It is known that stone was removed for road making in the late nineteenth century.

The mound is surrounded by an impressive ditch and bank, the former averaging 5.5m wide and up to 2.5m deep. Masonry once visible on the inside of the ditch at its north-west quarter suggests that it was lined with stone. The outer bank, formed from material thrown up from the ditch, is clearly visible and stands up to 4.0m wide and 0.5m high on most sides except the south-east where it no longer survives.

To the north and north-east of the mound are earthworks and ditches which may represent the boundaries of the bailey. There are also traces of ditches, enclosures and platforms in the fields nearby which mark the location of the vanished settlement which lay near the castle.

Ludlow Castle SO 508746 ★★★

Ludlow Castle is one of the great castles of England, the largest in the county and with a national as well as local significance. At the time of the Conquest, there was no settlement at Ludlow and the castle, begun after 1075, was the first building on the site. It was followed in the early twelfth century by the construction of a planned town, laid out to its south and east.

Unusually for Shropshire, Ludlow Castle was built in stone from the outset, the rocky site providing ample material. It stands in a fine defensive position on a limestone promontory, protected on three sides by cliffs over 30m high and with extensive views, especially to the north. It also commanded the crossing of the Teme. At the time of Domesday, the area was part of the manor of Stanton 'in Corvedale', held by the de Lacys, who gave their name to the manor as Stanton Lacy. The earliest castle may have been built by Walter de Lacy *c.*1075 or (more probably) by his successor, Roger de Lacy, who inherited the manor in 1085. After his exile in 1095, the castle was granted to Joce de Dinan who probably completed the initial work on the fortifications.

First referred to when besieged by King Stephen in 1139, it was again besieged in 1156 by Gilbert de Lacy on behalf of Henry II. Briefly in royal hands under Henry II and King John, it was restored to the de Lacy's in 1216.

After 1225 the town itself was encircled by stone walls, fragments of which remain in buildings round the town. Of its original gateways, the south gate with its D-shaped flanking towers survives as 'Broad Gate'. In 1314, the castle passed to Roger Mortimer, who with Queen Matilda briefly ruled England from the deposition of Edward II in 1326 until his own fall and execution in 1330. In 1424, the castle passed to Richard, Duke of York, and thereafter became involved in the conflict later known the 'Wars of the Roses'. The castle was severely damaged when occupied by the Lancastrians in 1459 and was repaired by Edward IV.

The castle's later significance lay in its role as the location of the Council of Wales and the Marches – the body responsible for enforcing royal law in Wales and the borderlands. Established at Ludlow Castle by Edward IV in 1471, it was reconstituted in 1501 and 1565. The Council was an important department of government, especially after the Union with Wales, 1536-43, and its Lords President were important figures. As Lord President in the late sixteenth century Sir Henry Sidney undertook a complete refurbishment of the medieval castle, creating a grand residence with suites of offices and apartments befitting the castle's status as a major administrative and legal centre. The Council was dissolved in 1641 and

82 The Norman chapel in Ludlow castle

83 An aerial view of Ludlow Castle, clearly showing the inner bailey (bottom centre) and the large outer bailey. *CPAT-92-MB-557*

84 The Inner Bailey of Ludlow castle, with the solar block (left), the Great Hall (centre) and the Great Chamber block *c.*1320 (right)

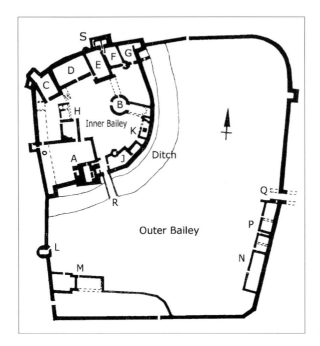

85 Plan of Ludlow Castle

although revived in the Restoration in 1660 it was abolished in 1689 and with its demise Ludlow Castle ceased to have a national role for the first time in centuries and slowly fell into ruin. (Lettered references in the text below refer to the plan of the castle)

The original castle comprised a roughly oval walled enclosure (later the inner bailey) on the north end of the promontory, dominated by a stone gatehouse tower (A) of the late eleventh century. Through this ran the original entrance to the castle. The bailey wall, up to 2.5m thick, was additionally defended by four square towers and protected to its south and east by a dry rock-cut ditch, which is still an impressive feature at over 3m deep and up to 12m wide (*colour plates 10* and *30*).

Apart from the keep, the finest survival of the earliest phase is the circular nave of the chapel of St Mary Magdalene (B). Modelled on the church of the Holy Sepulchre in Jerusalem (*c.*1099), it is one of only seven surviving circular Norman churches in England. The chapel was divided into two storeys in the late sixteenth century and doors cut into its new upper floor, connecting to the nearby apartments via a wooden gallery. Of its chancel, rebuilt in timber in the 1580s, only the foundations remain visible.

A major enlargement began *c*.1160 under Hugh de Lacy. The gatehouse tower was heightened to form the great keep (A) – one of the first of its kind in Shropshire – and the gateway through it was blocked. Its infilling is clearly visible, as are the stone supports for the bridge which gave access to it. A new gateway was cut through the south wall adjoining the keep, though the present bridge (R) dates to the late sixteenth century. The keep was much deeper at one time – its north wall is a late fifteenth-century reconstruction and excavations revealed that it originally extended 7m further north. The keep, raised to five storeys, contained a number of small rooms and garderobes, its lowest level (behind the blocked gateway) once used as a prison. The bedroom and garderobe block (S) projecting from the north wall may also date from this phase.

The Norman 'Pendover Tower' (G) at the north-east angle of the bailey has been greatly altered. It was said to have been occupied by Edward V and his brother Richard and much that now stands is the result of fifteenth-century alteration (e.g. the ground floor windows in the north wall) and of the late sixteenth-century refurbishment. To its west is a block (F) once used as an armoury and strong-room. Altered in the late sixteenth century, its upper rooms were used as additional lodgings.

The well in the inner bailey sinks to a depth of over 40m to the River Teme – a safe supply of water in time of siege. Of the domestic buildings, like the brew house and kitchen (H) which stood nearby, only foundations remain.

The rebuilding of *c*.1160 doubled the size of the castle by the creation of an outer bailey, which encroached into the town, with a curtain of stone walls up to 2m thick and 11m high. This was defended on the town side by a ditch, mostly now filled in, and entered through the east wall by the present gateway (Q), which as it stands looks rather weak as the main entrance to such an important castle. The house to the north of the main gate was built in the eighteenth century; it was briefly the residence of the exiled Emperor Napoleon III.

The D-shaped 'Mortimer Tower' on the west wall of the outer bailey (L) may belong to the time of Walter de Lacy *c*.1200 but was remodelled *c*.1300; it is named after one of the Mortimer lords of Wigmore once held prisoner there. It has two upper floors containing small chambers but in its basement, somewhat strangely, was a vaulted gateway with a portcullis until it was blocked in the sixteenth century.

Rebuilding on a grand scale occurred between 1285-1320 under Peter de Geneville (d.1292) and Roger Mortimer, and saw the construction against the north wall of the inner bailey of a palatial range of apartments – the Great Hall flanked by the solar block and the Great Chamber (C,D,E).

The solar block (C) was the first of the three to be constructed and dates to 1280-1300. It was the main residential unit until the completion of the Great Hall and Great Chamber in the 1320s. It is believed that Prince Arthur and Katherine of Aragon stayed here in 1501-02 until Arthur's death from the plague then ravaging Ludlow. The solar itself lay on the first floor and extended at its north-west corner into an earlier tower on the north wall. Above lay a suite of bedrooms and below it in the undercroft were servants' quarters or storerooms. Like so much else in the castle, it was remodelled in the late sixteenth century and was divided into smaller rooms.

The central building, the Great Hall (D), dates to the 1320s. Its lowest level was a storeroom, originally lit by four openings in the south wall. Above it lay the Great Hall, the social heart of the medieval castle, originally heated by an open central hearth. The hall, entered by a fine flight of stairs, had three large windows in its south wall, the central one blocked during the late sixteenth century when a fireplace was added to the room. Against the east interior wall was a raised dais. The roof was a massive wooden structure, whose corbels remain in situ, with a lantern over the central hearth to allow the upward flow of smoke. It was in this hall that one of the most famous events in Ludlow's history occurred when, at Michaelmas 1634, the masque *Comus* was first performed. With text by John Milton and music by William Lawes, it was a grand occasion celebrating the arrival of the Earl of Bridgwater as Lord President. The kitchens which served the hall and apartments stood in the bailey, immediately opposite the staircase, behind the keep. Only the foundations remain (H).

The Great Chamber block (E) served as the private apartments of the lord in medieval times and was the residence, for example, of Roger Mortimer, who completed the buildings in the 1320s. As usual, the lowest level was a dark storeroom, with the chamber above and private rooms over that. The main chamber became in due course the State Apartment of the President of the Council and was extensively altered in the late sixteenth century.

During the occupation of Roger Mortimer after 1314, the chapel of St Peter was built at the south-west angle of the outer bailey (M) and consecrated in 1328. Converted in the late sixteenth century, its new upper storey became the Court House or 'Hall of Justice' and its lower level a record office.

The final phase of rebuilding occurred in the 1580s under the Presidency (1559-86) of Sir Henry Sidney. Sir Henry, formerly Ambassador to France, was the father of the courtier and poet, Sir Philip Sidney, who grew up in Ludlow Castle. Sir Henry oversaw the conversion of the castle from a medieval fortress to an impressive office of state and grand residence. It had to be substantial to accommodate the large staff and retinue of the Council – four Judges, an attorney, lawyers, secretaries, clerks, counsellors, other officers and their attendants. Many of the buildings were altered during the period 1560-90 and new work included the Judges' Lodgings (completed 1581) to the east of the inner gateway (J), which bears the arms of Sir Henry below those of Elizabeth I. Its rooms are smaller than some of the grander rooms in the earlier castle (*colour plate 9*).

The laundry, in the inner bailey east of the Lodgings (K), and a decorative fountain have gone, as have buildings in the outer bailey, most of which would have been in timber. The porter's lodge next to the main gate (P), a prison and the stable range (N) along the east wall are of the late Tudor rebuild.

During the Civil War the castle was the principal seat of the Royalist cause in Shropshire, its sympathies reinforced by Parliament's abolition of the Council in 1641 – it had brought a great deal of trade and wealth to the town. During the war, the King and his nephews, Prince Rupert and Prince Maurice, stayed at Ludlow at various times.

Although there were Parliamentary raids in the vicinity of the town, it was deemed too strong for an outright attack to be launched against it and not until near the end of the war was it directly threatened. The fall of Shrewsbury to the north and Hereford to the south in 1645 isolated Ludlow and in April 1646 the Parliamentary commander Colonel Birch was ordered to capture the castle and town. He arrived on 24 April 1646 with approximately 1,000 men drawn from local garrisons and faced a Royalist garrison of only 350 under Sir Michael Woodhouse. The suburbs of Ludlow were occupied and the walled town and castle put under siege. When Birch left for Leominster to meet his heavy artillery, en route from Gloucester, Sir Michael attempted a raid on the besieging army but Birch was warned in advance and routed Woodhouse's force at Eyton. After the failure of another attempt by Woodhouse's cavalry to break out, negotiations led to the surrender of the town and castle on 1 June 1646. It was probably the mere threat of siege artillery which precipitated the collapse of the defence. In the event, the heavy artillery was not employed, although gun positions were prepared on ground overlooking the town on Whitcliffe Common, where their traces may still be seen.

At the Restoration in 1660, Charles II appointed Prince Rupert as the new Lord President but when the Council was abolished by William III in 1689 Ludlow ceased to have any national or royal function.

Fortunately, the castle was never subjected to a deliberate slighting and the roofing, lead and timbers were only removed during the period 1715-75. The result is a castle of great antiquity and significance which has been well preserved, without the major damage or alteration which others have suffered. Purchased by the Earl of Powis in 1811, it remains part of the family estates and is open to the public.

Lydbury North SO 351860

The house known as 'The Firs' in Lydbury North (only metres from the west door of the church of St Michael and All Angels) stands on a low, rectangular mound which has been variously interpreted as the remains of a Saxon earthwork, a moated site or a motte. There is no clear evidence for any of these and its origins remain conjectural.

Lydham Motte and Bailey SO 334910 ★

Before 1086, Lydham was one of the border holdings of Edric 'the Wild'. Though he acknowledged William I as overlord in 1066 and retained his lands after the conquest, he proved to be a troublesome vassal. Edric was involved in the Welsh attack on Hereford in 1067 and attacked the king's new castle at Shrewsbury in 1069. Nevertheless, he submitted to William in 1070 and is last heard of in 1072. His manor of Lydham was granted to Earl Roger, whose subtenant Edric became, and through Roger Lydham became part of the Honour of Montgomery.

It is not known who constructed the castle whose well-defined remains stand 200m north-west of Lydham church. Built at the confluence of the Rivers Onny and Camlad, it was defended by watercourses on three sides and was strategically located at the convergence of major east–west and north–south valley routes.

86 The motte at Lydham

The roughly oval mound, which has no visible ditch, is approximately 36 x 25m at its base, standing over 3m above ground level. The summit is roughly rectangular and approximately 16 x 9m. The bailey is defined by a bank, whose substantial remains to the west stand to a height of up to 2.5m, and the remains of a surrounding ditch up to 7m wide and 2.5m deep on all but the east side. There are entrances to the south-east and west of the site, both of which retain traces of the earthworks which defended their approaches. Within the bailey to the north-east and east are the remains of platforms on which the domestic buildings presumably stood.

Marche Hall Ringwork SJ 243107

After the Conquest, the manor of Marche (or Marshe) was divided between the Corbets of Caus and the Botterells, lords of Longden; the de Mersse (Marche) family were subtenants of both parts. On a prominent north-facing ridge 500m north-east of Marche Hall, and about 2km north-west of Westbury, lie the eroded remains of a ringwork. Now less than 2m high and extending to 35 x 26m, it commands extensive views in all directions, especially to the north. Slight traces of the surrounding ditch are visible only on its western side, where it is followed by the hedge line, but there are no

87 The very eroded remains of the ringwork at Marche

signs of a bailey, which may have lain to the north. Although now isolated in the landscape, it has been suggested that the castle was close to the vanished hamlet of Brerelawe.

Marton Motte and Bailey SJ 290026

Little remains of the motte and bailey which stood on the western side of Marton Pool near Chirbury. In 1086, the manor was one of seven owned by St Chad's in Shrewsbury and was held of the church by Alward. After the rebellion of 1102 and Henry I's seizure of a number of Shropshire manors, Marton became part of the Honour of Montgomery, held by the de Boulers family and later, during the reign of John, by the Cantilupes.

The castle was probably built in the late eleventh century, presumably after 1086. It was originally right on the lake – now greatly reduced – and its large bailey, lying to the south-west, seems to have been weakly defended on the side protected by the pool. The original mound ('The Mount') was about 5m high, with a summit diameter of only 6m and was typical of the small

88 The site of the motte at Marton, now occupied by the house at the rear right, with 'The Old School' to its left

castles built in the Vale of Montgomery, held by minor tenants during the early phase of Norman expansion towards Wales.

In Victorian times the village school (now 'The Old School') was built into the bailey, but the rest of the motte and much of the bailey were destroyed as recently as 1968 when a house was built on the site. All that remains is part of the bailey to the south-west, with slight traces of its ditch to the west and its bank and ditch to the north.

Meole Brace Castle SJ 487105

Meole Brace, once a separate manor, is now virtually a suburb of Shrewsbury. It was held by the Mortimers, with the de Bracey family (who gave the village its name) as tenants in the twelfth century.

There is a long tradition of a castle at Meole Brace but it is likely that the building was a fortified manor house built by the de Braceys rather than an actual castle; there are several references from 1273 to a house and 'tower' which may be the origin of the tradition. The house passed to the Zouche family in 1490 and then through various hands; it was presumably where Elizabeth I stayed in Meole on one occasion when her visit to Shrewsbury was diverted by an outbreak of plague. What was known as 'the castle house' was destroyed by fire during the reign of Charles II and although traces of its stonework were visible in the grounds of Meole Hall as late as *c.*1870 only fragments now remain. It stood immediately to the east of the church of Holy Trinity, on the west bank of a branch of the Rea Brook and close to a nearby crossing.

Middlehope Motte SO 499886

In 1086, Middlehope, a small, isolated settlement south of Wenlock Edge, was held of Earl Roger by Roger de Lacy and of him by Herbert, who also held Corfton (q.v.). It passed from Herbert to the de Furches family and from them to the de Middlehopes. The castle was presumably intended to dominate the upper end of the valley in which it sits.

The remains of the small motte and bailey lie in pastureland north-east of the village and are bisected by a farm road. The motte, now only 1m high, with a diameter of approximately 13m, has been much eroded and lies to the west of the road. Its bailey lay to the east, across the road, and is represented by a clear platform approximately 50m in diameter. There are traces of the bailey ditch to the south, where it is up to 10m wide and 1.2m deep. What may have been the original entrance lies on the east side of the bailey and there are remains of earthwork banks to the north-west and south-west. A circular platform to the north-west of the motte and another in the bailey may indicate the sites of buildings.

Middleton Motte SO 539773

Middleton stands on the B4364, 4km north-east of Ludlow. In the grounds at the entrance to Middleton Court and opposite the originally Norman church stands a damaged mound which may have been a motte. It has a 'stepped' appearance, with two 'peaks', one approximately 3.5m high and the other, only a few metres to its east, less than 2m high. This may be an elongated motte which has been dug away in the centre or which was later landscaped as part of a garden. In 1086, the manor was held of Earl Roger by William Pandolf (or Pantulf) and later by the de Higfords but nothing is known of a castle on this site.

89 The low remains of the motte at Middlehope; its bailey lay on the other side of the modern farm road running to the right

90 Tree-covered remains of the motte at Middleton Court in Middleton near Ludlow

91 The overgrown castle mound in the village of Minton

Minton Motte SO 432906

Minton was directly held by Earl Roger in 1086 and was later associated with the guardianship of the forest of Long Mynd. It lies in the foothills of the Long Mynd, 1.5km south-west of Little Stretton, and its motte stands opposite manor Farm. The land falls steeply away to the east, giving outstanding views to the east and north. Now very overgrown, the motte is 5m high with a summit diameter of 10-12m, but its ditch is visible only on the south-west and north-east sides and all remains of its bailey have gone. Given the fall of the land, it may have lain where the modern farm now stands.

More Motte and Bailey SO 339914 ★★

More does not feature in Domesday Book but lay within the manor of Lydham, which eventually became part of the Honour of Montgomery. Sometime during the reign of Henry I (1100-35), More became a separate manor in its own right.

Only 600m north-east of Lydham motte, the interesting site of More castle and its associated enclosures lies in marshy fields approximately 200m west of the twelfth-century church of St Peter. It occupies the western end of a tongue of land which protrudes into a marshy area from higher ground to its east. There is no clear strategic reason for its siting in this area but it is another local example of a castle-dominated planned settlement. Under Henry I, the manor was granted a charter by 'Grand Serjeanty' by which the lord of More was required to command 200 foot soldiers whenever the King crossed into Wales in time of war and to march in the van of the royal army, carrying the King's standard.

Excavation revealed that the motte began as a ringwork. Its centre was later filled in to create a mound which now stands only 2.5m high, with a flat summit about 20m in diameter. It is surrounded by a well-defined ditch, up to 9m wide, with an outer bank to its west, south and north.

To the east and north-east of the motte lie two sharply-defined banked and ditched enclosures, forming an inner and outer bailey. The inner bailey is approximately 58m square, though damaged on its south side, and retains traces of building platforms. The bailey ditch to the north-east is crossed by a causeway into the outer bailey, which is approximately 50 x 85m, and bounded by slopes to the north and south and banks to the west and east. A trackway crosses the outer bailey and runs for approximately 200m to join the modern road north-west of the church. A possible third enclosure, lying still further to the east, is ill-defined where it abuts the marshy ground and could represent part of the medieval village. Around the site are other traces of the settlement which lay near the castle, in the form of ridge and furrow features, fishponds, earthworks etc (*colour plate 12*).

92 The low earthworks of the bailey at More; the church and the modern village are visible in the background

Pottery of the twelfth and thirteenth centuries has been found on the site, which *may* be the location of *Matefelun* and/or the castle of *Moretoin*; the former occurs in a reference in 1195 and the later in 1215.

Moreton Corbet Castle SJ 561231 ★★★

The ruins of Moreton Corbet, with its attached Renaissance mansion, form one of the most picturesque of Shropshire's castle sites. At the time of Domesday, *Mortone* was held by Thorold de Verley, one of 13 manors he held of Earl Roger. These holdings became known as the Fee of Chetwynd and passed to the Fitz Alans. The manor's tenants in the twelfth century were the Toret family, the village being known as Moreton Toret (or Turret) as late as 1516 – long after their connection with it had ceased in 1230, when it passed by marriage to the Corbets of Wattlesborough. The settlement which developed around the castle was inhabited into the early sixteenth century (when Leland recorded 'the faire castell of Mr. Corbettes'), but was deserted by the time the castle was remodelled after 1570. Only a scattering of houses and the nearby church of St Bartholomew (*c*.1140) now remain.

93 The remains of the keep (*c*.1200) at Moreton Corbet, with part of the curtain wall visible in the background

94 The late sixteenth-century Renaissance range at Morteton Corbet from the west. The entire north wall has gone (see also *colour plate 13*)

The Torets presumably built the first castle on the site, now vanished, but identified as a small keep at one side of a low platform surrounded by a wooden palisade and moat. The present square keep may have been built by Bartholomew Fitz Toret *c.*1200. Extending to 12 x 9m, its walls are 1.7m thick and stand to a height of two (formerly three) storeys. Set on a chamfered plinth with pilaster buttresses, only its north face and fragments of the east and west walls survive. It is not unlike the tower at Wattlesborough (q.v.) which was owned by the Corbet family who held Moreton Corbet after 1230. Its lower storey would have been a dark storeroom, with a hall above, in which are the remains of a fireplace.

The Corbets of Wattlesborough may have completed the reconstruction of the castle in stone, including a curtain wall with a gatehouse in its northern side. Roughly triangular in plan, the castle was built in local sandstone with ashlar dressings. Parts of the curtain wall, which was reconstructed in the sixteenth century, remain to some height between the keep and the two-storeyed gatehouse and between that and the east range. The gatehouse was remodelled in the fourteenth century and again during the late sixteenth century; a window on the upper floor bears the date '1579' and the 'elephant and castle' device of the Corbets. The walls show the scars of later buildings which have now vanished, in the form of roof lines, fireplaces, latrines and windows. The castle was surrounded by a moat, traces of which are visible as a depression up to 15m wide around all but the south side, where it was filled in during the late sixteenth century rebuilding. It was crossed by a causeway in front of the gatehouse.

The east range was restructured in the early sixteenth century and was set along a different alignment from the original curtain, with a great hall at its southern end which encroached on the earlier moat. In the 1570s, it was again altered and incorporated into the new house then being built.

A massive rebuilding began in the 1570s under the auspices of Sir Andrew Corbet (d.1579), who served as Sheriff of Shropshire on several occasions, and was continued by his son, Robert. They began to create an elaborate L-shaped Italianate mansion, built into the south side of the castle, though slightly further south than the original line of the walls and overlying part of the moat.

The architect of this ostentatious new house, which bears the date '1579', is not known but it might have been Robert Corbet himself. As a diplomat, he travelled extensively throughout Europe; Camden recorded that he was 'carried away with the affectionate delight of architecture' and began 'a most gorgeous and stately house, after the Italian model'. However, he never lived to see his plans fulfilled and when he died of the plague in 1583 much of the work was incomplete. The new mansion, which incorporated the recently rebuilt east range, housed a suite of large, square chambers. Approximately 52m long by 10m wide, it was built of sandstone lined with brick on the interior and with fine-quality ashlar facings on the outside.

The north side, which overlooked the 'courtyard' facing the revamped gatehouse and would no doubt have incorporated an imposing, decorated entrance, has largely gone. The south side (*colour plate 13*) has a symmetrical facade with three projecting bays, each with five-light mullion and transom windows; its shaped gables carry three-light windows with triangular pediments. The house must have had spacious and high rooms with a light interior. The facade is decorated with Doric pillars to the ground floor and Ionic to the first, the storeys being separated by a decorative frieze and with carved pedestals bearing beasts at the corners. Small doorways in the bays are framed with caryatids with Ionic capitals supporting entablatures with uncarved medallions. In the brick-lined interior fragmentary remains of decorative features, such as moulded surrounds and cornices, are visible, as are some of the fireplaces. The parapet, carrying obelisks with figures (most of which have gone) and its shaped gables would have given the house a very distinctive skyline.

Elaborate gardens associated with the new mansion extended to the south, visible from the great windows, and some of the landscaping features are still vaguely discernible. Here in the 1570s were an orchard, arbours, covered walks, gazebos and formal gardens which must have added considerably to the elegance of the mansion. West of Castle Farm the remains of a causeway may represent the original access to the mansion, with earthworks on either side recalling garden features which ornamented the approach to the house.

At the time of the Civil War, the castle was owned by Sir Vincent Corbet and held a Royalist garrison by the end of 1643. It is reported to have been well-fortified, with windows and doorways blocked to resist attack. However, Moreton Corbet stood siege only briefly before it fell on the 20 September 1644 to Parliamentary forces under Lieut. Col. Reinking, the German mercenary who was instrumental in the taking of Shrewsbury in 1645. It was occupied by a Parliamentary garrison until the end of the war, when its fortifications were destroyed.

Sir Vincent Corbet sold the house to pay his Civil War fines and although it was bought back by Andrew Corbet in 1743, plans for its completion or reconstruction were never carried out. Designs for rebuilding the house by John Haycock are known as late as 1796 but were never executed. The south range was roofless by 1776 and the site had reached its present condition by the mid-nineteenth century. It remains in the ownership of the Corbet family though it is now under the stewardship of English Heritage.

Myddle Castle sj 468236

Myddle is an interesting village, whose more recent history was recorded by Richard Gough in his famous *History of Myddle*, published in 1701. In 1086 it was held of Earl Roger by Reginald de Bailleul, Sheriff of Shropshire, as one of many held by this important official. Its church and tithes were granted to Shrewsbury Abbey before 1086 but by the thirteenth century most of the manor's lands were held by the Fitz Alans and passed from them to the le Strange family of Knockin.

The site lies at Castle Farm off the Myddle–Morton road, about 100m east of the medieval church of St Peter. It was occupied before 1308, in which year John le Strange received from Edward II licence to crenellate his moated mansion at Myddle. It passed briefly to the Kynaston family in the mid-fifteenth century and then to the Earls of Derby *c*.1482. Even by then the castle was in decay and was described as 'veri ruinus' by Leland in the 1540s. In the late sixteenth century, Myddle castle passed to the Egertons (later Earls of Bridgwater) and though they may have carried out some repairs, they never lived there. Richard Gough, in his *History of Myddle* makes no reference to the use of the castle during the Civil War but does record the collapse of many of the remaining buildings in an earthquake in 1688. A stone on the site records repairs by the Egertons as late as 1849.

Gough gives us a useful description of what was essentially a rectangular 'courtyard' castle in its last years. It stood within a wide moat, with an outer

95 The solitary standing fragment of the castle of Myddle – part of the of the hall's north-east stairwell tower

enclosure to its east, protected by a narrower moat. This 'bailey' was entered through a gatehouse at its north-east corner, the gateway being 8ft wide. There were four rooms in the gatehouse, two of which Gough could remember in use a bakery. He also recalls one building used as a slaughterhouse. This implies that however ruinous, Myddle castle performed some local function well into the seventeenth century. The bailey moat carried a bridge leading to the castle itself and a passageway led into the courtyard, which was surrounded by ranges of buildings. Gough records a possible kitchen and 'a pleasant roome, supposed to be a parlour' in the south range. The hall lay at the west of the courtyard, a fragment of its north-east stairwell tower being the only part of the stone structure to remain visible. Gough recalls that the castle was two storeys high, with a flat roof, but with a tower at the north-west corner of the courtyard.

The moated castle, probably much altered over generations, would have been an imposing sight, but all that remains of its buildings is a forlorn finger of red sandstone. Despite being strengthened in 1849, a large part of this fragment collapsed as recently as 1976. Stretches of wall, with fine dressed stone, and other foundations have been found in excavations on the site (e.g. in 1966). The platform which bore the main buildingss is about 2m above the remains of the moat and covers an area approximately 44 x 49m. Although farm buildings and a yard have been built over the moat against the eastern section of its retaining wall, the main platform, its moat (now largely filled in) and the bailey to the east remain identifiable.

Newcastle Motte so 244821

The remains of a small motte known as 'The Crugyn' lie in the valley of the River Clun, about 500m south-west of the church in Newcastle. It is presumably the 'new castle' after which the village was named. An impressive section of Offa's Dyke passes about 1km to the east. Along with Llanhedrick, Bicton, Whitcott and Keysett, Newcastle was part of 'the Manor of the Five Towns', within the powerful Barony of Clun, held initially by the de Says and then by the Fitz Alans.

The motte is about 20m in diameter with a summit 7 x 5m and is 3m high. There are no visible remains of a bailey or of associated earthworks and ditches and nothing is known of its history.

96 The insignificant castle mound on the River Clun at Newcastle. No trace of any bailey remains

Oswestry Castle SJ 292298 ★

The border town of Oswestry, named after its shrine to the Northumbrian king St Oswald, who was martyred nearby in AD 624, became an important market town and frontier base. After 1086 it displaced nearby Maesbury as the local centre and eventually became the main holding of the Fitz Alan barony and the hub of a Marcher lordship in its own right.

Domesday Book refers to the castle – one of only three references to Shropshire castles, the others being Shrewsbury and Holdgate – and states that it was built by Rainald (Reginald) de Bailleul, Sheriff of Shropshire, who held the manor of his kinsman Earl Roger. It has been suggested that the earliest castle was the work of Warin 'the Bald' (d.1085) who preceded Reginald as Sheriff, but Domesday implies that the castle was Reginald's construction. Interestingly, the castle in its earliest days was known as Luvre or Loure, a corruption of the Early French *l'uuvre*, (modern *l'oeuvre*) meaning a 'work' or fortification.

The large motte which remains, now landscaped and part of the town park, stands 9-10m high with a base of 70m in diameter and offers commanding views in all directions. The flat summit extending to 20 x 32m, bears three mutilated fragments, 2.5m thick, of a polygonal shell keep. This may have been constructed by Madog ap Meredith, Prince of Powys, who took the castle from William Fitz Alan in 1148 or was built in a reconstruction

97 Masonry fragments remaining in situ on the summit of the motte at Oswestry

98 Print of *c.*1770 by Dukes, showing substantial buildings still standing on the motte at Oswestry – which implies that its slighting in the seventeenth century was by no means complete

*c.*1155 by William once he had regained control. Taken by King John in 1212, the castle was recaptured by John Fitz Alan in 1214 and withstood a royal attack which burned the town in 1216. As at Shrewsbury, the castle served as a base during Edward I's Welsh campaign in 1277. In 1398 Oswestry Castle was the venue for the Parliament moved from Shrewsbury by Richard II and a contemporary inquisition listed its rooms as the wardrobe, buttery, Great Chamber, Middle Chamber, Constable's Hall, chapel of St Nicholas, kitchen and larder.

After *c.*1280 town walls in stone were built as a defence against Welsh attacks (such as that which again burned the town in 1263). These ran from the motte at its south-west and north-east faces. The walls have now gone, though their course can be traced, and the town gates which pierced them are recalled in street names like Willow Gate, Beatrice Gate, New Gate, Black Gate etc. What remained of the gates was demolished between 1771-83.

All visible traces of the two baileys which lay east and south of the motte have vanished, though their location is reflected in street names like 'Bailey Street' and 'Bailey Head' and in the alignment of Leg Street, Cross Street and Willow Street. Sections of earth rampart and ditches have been located during excavations in the town, as have traces of the ditch which surrounded the motte. The south bailey seems to have been the original site of the town which grew in the shadow of the castle.

By the time of Leland's visit, the castle 'set on a mount' was still standing and 'dichid' to its south-west, where the town walls joined the defences. It had remained, with only brief periods of loss, in Fitz Alan ownership until 1595, but by 1603, when it was granted to Thomas Howard, Earl of Suffolk, it was recorded as being in poor repair. From the Howards, the castle eventually passed to the Earls of Powis.

An important border town defended by its castle and town walls, Oswestry was held for the king in 1642. Attacked by Parliamentary forces under Colonel Mytton on 23 June 1644, the garrison was driven back into the castle and when its gates were blown in with gunpowder, they quickly negotiated a surrender. An immediate Royalist attempt to recapture the town, employing 5,000 troops from Shrewsbury and other local garrisons, was defeated after severe fighting and Oswestry became, with Wem, a centre of Parliamentary activity in the county. In 1647, Parliament decreed that its fortifications be slighted.

Although the castle is reported to have been demolished after the Civil War, eighteenth-century prints imply that significant parts of the structure escaped demolition and were retained for residential or administrative use. The motte was incorporated into an ornamental park in 1852 and the site taken over by the town council in 1890.

Pan Castle SJ 526404 ★

Pan Castle is an unusual site. A low but extensive motte (approximately 58 x 45m) is surrounded by a well-defined ditch, up to 15m wide in places and often water-filled. It looks very like a moated manor house site, except that to its south and west are the remains of large earth banks and deep ditches which may represent part of the boundaries of a large, irregular bailey. The castle stands on a bank projecting into low-lying fields which are marshy in wet weather and could have been partly defended by its marshy surroundings.

Pan Castle may have been constructed after the Conquest by William de Warenne, who held the manor of Whitchurch 2km to the north-west and may have built the castle there, or between 1135-90 by the Fitz Ranulfs, a branch of the de Warennes. A reference to repairs in 1119 may relate to Pan Castle or to Whitchurch but otherwise little is known about the site. No masonry survives and excavations early in the twentieth century revealed only timber fragments. It has been suggested that the castle was abandoned in favour of Blakemere (q.v.) by its later tenants, the le Strange family, in the early fourteenth century.

99 The wide ditch or moat at Pan Castle, with the low, rectangular motte to right

100 The tree-covered mound (right) on the slopes of the hill at Pennerley. Viewed from what may be the bailey site

Pennerley Mound SO 351994

A fine round barrow known as 'The Knapp' crowns the summit of Round Hill at Pennerley. About 150m further down the hill lies an elongated high mound whose origins are disputed. Some authorities regard it as a natural feature or another burial mound, but the consensus seems to be that it is a motte, perhaps adapting a natural feature. It stands approximately 5m high with a base diameter of 25m and has been partially cut into by the construction of a cottage on its south-east face. The faint outline of what may be a bailey extends to the north of the mound, marked by possible boundary banks. Natural or not, it commands superb views in all directions, especially towards the Stiperstones to its east and the valleys to its north.

Petton Motte SJ 441262

In 1086, Petton was one of six manors held of Earl Roger by his retainer, Robert 'the Butler'. After the rebellion of 1102 all were forfeited to the Crown and became part of the Honour of Montgomery.

There is some doubt as to the nature of the large mound which stands less than 100m south-east of the small church, which replaced an original of

101 The mound at Petton, showing part of the extensive damage to the south-east of the site

c.1159. It has been considered to be a Bronze Age burial mound, a motte or simply a gazebo base associated with Petton Hall. The main mound stands up to 2m high and 12m across, with a lower mound at its south-west which houses a later brick ice-house. The site offers good all-round views, especially to the east. Although there is no evidence of a bailey, the area has been badly dug away to the south-east, so that it is difficult to distinguish between possibly early features and the effects of more recent quarrying for gravel. Indeed, erosion and land slip to the south-east face of the motte threaten the stability and survival of the mound itself.

Pickthorne Castle SO 669840

The small manor of Pickthorne (or Pickthorn) was held from Saxon times by St Milburga's, the Priory Church of Much Wenlock. Established before AD 690, the Priory was refounded by Earl Roger *c*.1080 and linked ultimately to the great Abbey of Cluny. Domesday Book confirms that Pickthorn was in the hands of the Priory and it later joined other holdings of St Milburga's as part of the Liberty of Wenlock.

The remote site known as 'The Castle' lies in marshy ground near Pickthorn Farm, 1km north-north-west of Stottesdon church, and is bounded by streams

102 The low motte at Pickthorne (left) with part of its wide surrounding moat and low outer bank

to its east and south. It may be the location of the mansion of the Baskerville family referred to *c.*1284 and resembles the site of a moated manor house. The irregular mound, whose western half has recently been planted with saplings, measures approximately 56 x 34m, and stands in places up to 2m above the bottom of the dry moat. The wide moat and low outer bank which surrounded the mound are most clearly visible to the east of the site and enclose another raised platform, possibly a bailey, lying to the south-east. No trace of any stonework remains.

Pont Fadoc Motte sj 292211

Near the bridge of Pont Fadoc (or Fadog), 3.5km west of Kinnersely, is a very low, roughly circular mound which has been tentatively identified as a motte. It is 26m in diameter but less than 1m high and lies in marshy ground on the banks of the Morda stream where it is crossed by the modern B4398. There are faint traces of a ditch on the north-east side of the mound, but the location of its bailey is unknown and nothing is known of its history.

Above: 1 Acton Burnell
castle and church from
the north-west

Right: 1a The interior
of the north-west
tower at Acton Burnell,
showing windows
and doorways in the
Bishop's apartments

2 The remains of the keep at Bridgnorth, with the church of St Mary Magdalene to the right

3 Broncroft Castle

4 Clun: the high platform of the south bailey, with its deep surrounding ditch

5 Clun: the motte and masonry remains from the east bailey

Above: 6 The motte and bailey at Hockleton: typical of the small castles in the Vale of Montgomery

Right: 7 The thirteenth-century tower incorporated into Holdgate farm

Left: 8 Decoration over the doorway in the Norman Chapel at Ludlow Castle

Below: 9 South wall of the inner bailey at Ludlow showing an early tower (left), the keep and gateway (centre) and the Judges' Lodgings (right)

Left: 10 The keep
at Ludlow, with the
infilling of the earlier
gateway clearly visible

Below: 11 The inner
bailey at Ludlow,
showing the Norman
chapel (right) and the
buildings ranges of
1280-1320

12 An aerial view of the site at More, clearly showing the motte (top left) with the baileys and enclosures adjacent to it. *CPAT*

13 The Renaissance block of *c.*1579 forming the south range at Moreton Corbet

14 The Hall of Shrewsbury Castle from the motte. Note the more recent low sandstone wall of the motte, standing on earlier foundations

15 Stokesay Castle viewed across the pond to its west, which once fed the moat

Left: 16 The stark outer face of the keep at Wattlesborough, with the remains of a fourteenth-century window

Below: 17 The remains at Whittington, viewed from the earlier motte. To the right are the ruins of the inner bailey and its gatehouse; to the left is the well-preserved gatehouse of the outer bailey with its adjoining cottage

Above: 18 Whittington viewed from across its surviving wet moats. To the left, the inner bailey and its one remaining gatehouse tower and to the right the D-shaped towers which guarded the entrance to the outer bailey

Left: 19 The powerful south tower at Stokesay, dated to the late thirteenth century

20 The large motte at Bishop's Moat, viewed from the bailey to the east

21 The east range at Cheney Longville, retaining some of its early doors and windows

22 The low motte at the centre of the extensive site at Culmington; the church of All Saints visible in the background to its right

23 Stokesay: exterior view of the north tower with its wooden jettied storey, the Hall range and the south tower

24 Bishop's Castle. The motte (the circular bowling green, bottom centre) and the shape of its bailey is clearly shown in this aerial photograph. The planned town stretches in linear fashion from the castle to the church (centre top). *CPAT-92-C-18*

25 Laura's Tower: the late eighteenth-century summerhouse standing on the base of a thirteenth-century watchtower on the motte at Shrewsbury

Opposite
Top: 26 The eroded site of the ringwork known as 'Caesar's Camp' near Wollaston; hardly anything now remains visible

Middle: 27 The remains of the curtain walls on the summit of the motte at Clun, with part of the tower (right)

Bottom: 28 The castle at Ellesmere commanded a fine view over the mere and the area to its south-east

Right: 29 The rock-cut ditch separating the inner bailey (right) from the outer bailey at Ludlow

Above: 30 The impressive motte at Wilmington viewed from the south

31 The sandstone Hall at Shrewsbury, from the Inner Bailey. The modern entrance (far right) is on the site of the original raised entrance and was restored in 1924

32 Pan Pudding Hill – an early siege work only 500m from Bridgnorth castle and used as a gun emplacement during the Civil War

Pontesbury Castle SJ 401058

The large manor of Pontesbury was held by the Corbets in 1086, passing from Roger Fitz Corbet to the Corbets of Caus. In the thirteenth century, its tenants were the Fitz Herbert family. Pontesbury seems to have been a large and important castle, but little remains visible. It stood south-east of the church of St George, a Saxon foundation, in the angle now formed by the junction of the Shrewsbury road with Chapel Street. The castle mound, some 60m in diameter, lay in the area now behind the United Reformed Chapel. Houses built to the west and south of the mound in the 1960s hemmed in what was left of the site so that all that remains visible are a few plots of open land (modern gardens) where the mound with its great stone tower once stood.

Pontesbury is believed to have begun life as a ringwork, with a surrounding ditch, up to 2m deep, and a summit rampart. At a later stage (perhaps *c.*1180-1220), a large stone keep was built, up to 15m high and 18m square, whose massive foundations were located by excavation in the 1960s. This could have been the work of the Corbets or of their Fitz Herbert tenants who held

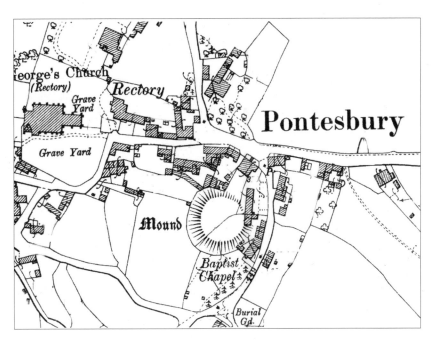

103 Map showing the location of Pontesbury Castle

the manor by the early thirteenth century. Pottery dated to 1150–1300 was found on the site and the indication is that Pontesbury was abandoned as early as *c.*1300 and may have been destroyed by fire. Substantial ruins survived into the 1540s when Leland recorded 'great tokens of stones fallen down' and fragments of the tower remained to be robbed of sandstone into the early nineteenth century. There was probably a large outer bailey whose site is now completely built over.

Quatford Motte and Bailey so 738908 ★

The settlement at Quatford on the River Severn, 3km south-east of Bridgnorth, is a fascinating site. A Saxon village may have existed here, as a *burh* founded by Aethelflaed *c.*912, though this could have been at Bridgnorth. What is certain is that by the time of Domesday, Earl Roger had acquired the manor of Eardington from Wenlock Priory and built at Quatford a collegiate church (endowed with the revenues of the manor), a borough and a 'new house' (*nova domus*). The 'new house' may be the castle itself (i.e. a fortified house) or a separate hall built as a residence for the Earl within the castle perimeters. As late as the 1540s, Leland could record that there 'yett appeare great tokens of a Pyle or Manour place' and in more recent times, large stone fragments which may have been the remains of this 'house' have been found on the bailey site.

Whatever its Saxon connections, Quatford was a planned Norman settlement. Tradition asserts that it was based around a church established by Earl Roger to fulfil a vow in return for the safe homecoming of his wife, but it is more likely to have been sited here to control a crossing point on the Severn and the important valley route. It is likely that the Severn was crossed just to the south by a Saxon bridge, since a *Cwatbrycg* is mentioned in 896 and a *Cantbricge* in 910. The foundation documents of the Earl's new church (St Mary Magdalene) also refer to a bridge. In 1101, Earl Roger's eventual successor, Robert of Bellême, recognising the greater strength of the site at Bridgnorth, transferred his seat to it and began the first castle there (q.v.). He did not have long to enjoy it, since his rebellion in 1102 resulted in the forfeiture of his Shropshire lands. However, with the move to Bridgnorth, Quatford lost its strategic significance and its castle was probably abandoned after less than 30 years in existence. The village presumably fell into decline at the same time and the nearby bridge may have been destroyed or removed,

104 Quatford: motte (right), ditch and bank from the east

since there is no further reference to it. A ferry remained in operation across the river to the south of the castle for generations.

Occupying a sandstone spur overlooking the Severn, the imposing oval motte stands 9m high and towers above the river when seen from the opposite bank, though parts have been eroded by the Severn. It now has a diameter of approximately 20 x 32m at its summit and is separated from its bailey to the east by an impressive rock-cut ditch which is over 9m wide in places and up to 2.5m deep. The bailey stands on a clear platform extending to 90 x 42m. It lay in the area between the motte and the church, but its eastern side has been damaged by work on the Kidderminster–Bridgnorth road. Excavation located post-holes but little in the way of dateable evidence; if it was only in occupation between c.1080 and 1101, there may be little left to find.

Red Castle sj 572295 ★★

Red Castle is an interesting site that deserves to be better known since it utilises natural features in a way which is seen nowhere else in the county. It presumably succeeded the castle at Weston (q.v.) which lies only 600m to its south-west. The manor, originally a Peverel holding, reverted to the Crown by 1130 and was held for a time by the le Strange family until it passed to the Audleys in the late twelfth century. Henry *de Aldithele*, Sheriff of Shropshire and Staffordshire, obtained the site from Maud le Strange in 1227 and was given licence in that year to erect at *Radeclif* a castle which became the principal Shropshire residence of this powerful family. In 1238, it was reported to be in good repair, but little is known of its subsequent history. It is thought to have been abandoned by 1386, following the death of James, lord Audley, and was purchased from the family by Henry VIII in 1536; Leland recorded that it was '… now al ruinus. It hath bene strong and hath decayed many a day'. The site passed to the Corbets in the late sixteenth century and may have played some role in the Civil War, briefly housing a Parliamentary garrison in 1645 and possibly holding prisoners of war. Red Castle passed to the Hill family of nearby Hawkstone Hall in the eighteenth century and its ruins were 'improved' as part the decorative landscape laid out in the Park in the 1780s. It now stands on the edge of the golf course at Hawkstone Park, in the tree-covered rocky outcrops directly opposite the hotel.

105 Mid-nineteenth-century view of Red Castle from the north, showing the remains of three towers

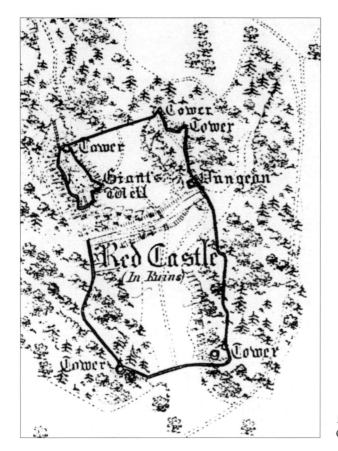

106 Plan of Red
Castle *c.*1880

The castle was begun in 1227 by Henry de Audley and skilfully incorporated
into its defences two high, parallel sandstone ridges as its western and eastern
'walls'. They stand about 90m apart and up to 18m high. Because of their natural strength and height, there was little need for further defences on these sides,
but the ridges were nevertheless topped with low shale parapets, of which fragments remain. On the northern tip of the western ridge there may have been a
small redoubt or keep at the most inaccessible section of the defences.

The open ends between the ridges were originally crossed by stone walls
(now largely gone) and created a roughly rectangular interior space approximately 160 x 92m, sloping from south to north. This space was divided into
two unequal baileys by a 3m-deep east–west rock-cut ditch with openings
cut through the cliff 'walls' to provide postern gates at either end. The larger

107 Fine dressed red sandstone at the base of the Well Tower. The tower, like everything else on this site, is totally obscured by vegetation

southern bailey, approximately 98 x 90m, had circular towers at its south-west and south-east corners. Both are now ruinous and completely overgrown but indicate a diameter of 8-9m and a wall thickness of about 2m. There were three towers in the smaller north bailey, one on the west ridge and two on the east, but these, too, are fragmentary and little remains to be seen. Marks and holes in the sandstone ridges may indicate the site of internal structures but nothing is left of them apart from rock-cut steps.

Standing against the west ridge in the north bailey is the most significant remnant – a well-tower surviving to a height of over 16m from the bailey floor to the top of the ridge. Constructed of fine red sandstone on a battered base, it houses an impressive rock-cut well a further 15m deep. Although sometimes regarded as a reconstruction associated with the follies at Hawkstone and known as 'the Giant's Well', the tower appears to be an authentic medieval structure, with original arrow slits and the indications of several floor levels, presumably accessed only by trap doors and ladders.

However, it too is so completely overgrown that, despite its height, it can be hard to locate on site.

Another interesting feature is the so-called 'dungeon', a deep rock-cut chamber in the sandstone wall of the south-east corner of the north bailey. Although it is also ascribed to the folly-building of the late eighteenth century, it must have been the product of considerable effort and it may have had some original function in the castle.

When the elaborate follies were constructed nearby in Hawkstone Park in the 1780s the ruins of Red Castle were undoubtedly 'tidied up' and even added to, to incorporate them into the 'romantic' landscape then being laid out. To make matters worse, any interpretation of the site is complicated by the fact that it is now – like Charlton, Brogyntyn and Ritton – so completely overgrown that access and an overall view are difficult at any time.

Ritton Castle SO 345977

Ritton does not occur in Domesday but lay in the manor of Wentnor, held by the Corbets of Caus. A manor of Ritton is first mentioned in 1203 when Robert Corbet gave the mill to Buildwas Abbey; its castle was presumably the *caput* or principal residence of the Corbets in the manor.

Ritton is remote and difficult of access. It lies on a projecting spur north-west of Brook's Hill, in heavily forested land. The site made good use of the lie of the terrain, which slopes steeply away from it in three directions, with additional defences added where required on the south-western and eastern sides. It commanded good views over the nearby valley and surrounding country.

The castle began life as an Iron Age hill-fort, about 115 x 215m, roughly rectangular in shape, with a single earth rampart, ditch and outer bank. Until recently, its outer bank stood to a height of up to 2-3m. In the early Middle Ages, the fort was adapted to create a ringwork and bailey. The triangular ringwork, covering approximately 32 x 28m, was formed by an east–west rampart and ditch cutting off the northern section of the old fort and was entered by a causeway on the southern side. The rest of the large hill-fort, covering over 1ha, presumably served as the bailey and was entered on its eastern side. It would have contained a range of domestic buildings and was large enough to support a sizeable community.

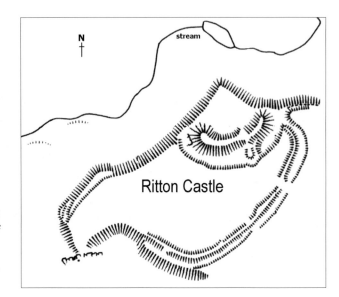

108 Plan of the earthworks at Ritton. Nothing like this is visible on site, the area now under forest and totally overgrown

Forestry work in the early 1960s levelled many of Ritton's banks and subsequent planting has completely obscured the site, so that it is now impossible to gain any overall impression. Scattered masonry fragments relate to the workings of the later Ritton Castle Mine.

Rorrington Motte sj 303004

At the time of Domesday, the manor of Rorrington was divided between Robert and Roger Fitz Corbet. It is not known who built the remote motte and bailey, whose mound stands on the slopes of Rorrington Hill above a steep-sided valley, which provided a defensive slope to its west. It commands extensive views in all directions, especially to the north and west towards the Rea Brook valley.

The motte is circular and very low – only about 2.5m above the surrounding land – with a flat top of a diameter of 16m. A clearly defined ditch, 2m wide and 0.5m deep in places, survives around the north-east side of the mound; it was not needed on the western face because of the natural fall of the land and to the south-east has been destroyed by the construction of a house ('The Mount') and other buildings. There is no trace of a bailey or perimeter defences.

109 The low castle mound, ditch and outer bank at Rorrington

Rowton Castle SJ 329128

The manor of Rowton was one of a number held in 1086 by Alward, son of Almund. With Amaston (see Heath Farm) it descended in the Honour of Montgomery. A castle possibly near the present site is referred to as early as 1282 and a deer park, owned by Bishop Robert Burnell, is recorded in 1292. But if the modern house stands on the site of the medieval castle, thought to have been destroyed by the Welsh, nothing remains of it. Another castle or house was built by the Lyster family in the 1460s. Saxton's map of 1577 shows the deer park with, at its south-west, what may be the 'old castle' mentioned in 1696 but it is thought that whatever existed at the time of the Civil War was slighted then or shortly afterwards. Rowton's owner at that time, Thomas Lyster, knighted for his financial contribution to the royal cause, was captured at Shrewsbury when it fell in February 1645 and it is believed that Rowton's garrison abandoned the castle immediately afterwards. There appears to be no foundation for the tradition that the castle's defence continued under Lady Lyster, who fought off an attack by Colonel Mytton. A new mansion was constructed on or near the site for Richard Lyster *c*.1700.

The present castle is largely a construction of the early nineteenth century (mainly 1809-12 and 1824-8), built around the core of Richard Lyster's brick

110 Rowton Castle, now a hotel and leisure centre

mansion. His descendant Colonel Henry Lyster commissioned the architect George Wyatt and others to refurbish the house in 'Gothick' style between 1809-28. Here and there earlier components were introduced into Wyatt's building to give it a 'period' flavour – for example, a thirteenth-century doorway, possibly from Alberbury Castle (q.v.), re-used in the stable court-yard. The castle, standing on the A458 Shrewsbury-Welshpool road, is now a hotel and leisure centre.

Ruckley Motte SO 532999

What may have been a flat-topped motte surrounded by a shallow ditch to the south of Ruckley village, near Acton Burnell, was levelled prior to 1971. Nothing visible remains.

Rushbury Ringwork SO 515919 ★

In 1086, Rushbury was held of Earl Roger by Roger de Lacy and from him by one Odo. The motte is a well-defined feature, lying at the edge of the village in 'Bury Field', less than 100m north–north-east of the late Saxon church of St Peter.

The mound is almost circular, standing to a height of up to 3m on its eastern side, with a summit diameter of approximately 45m. It is surrounded by a well-preserved ditch, nearly 10m wide in places, with the remains of a low outer bank. The location of its bailey is not known, though there are traces of earthworks in the field to its east.

111 The mound (left) of the ringwork at Rushbury, with ditch and outer bank to foreground

Ruyton XI Towns Castle SJ 393223

This strangely-named village is derived from the amalgamation of 11 'towns' to form one manor in the twelfth century. At Domesday, Ruyton itself was one of three manors held of Earl Roger by Odo de Bernières, 'the soldier' (*miles*), who granted lands to Shrewsbury Abbey early in the twelfth century. The manor passed to the Fitz Alans, becoming part of their lordship of Oswestry, and was held of them by the le Strange family.

The castle may have begun as a motte and bailey, possibly built after 1086 by John le Strange. Its builders chose a strong natural position on the western end of a low, narrow promontory overlooking the River Parry, with the bailey lying to the east and now occupied by the church and churchyard. The Victorian churchyard wall may mark the extent of the bailey compound.

A stone castle, possibly in existence by 1148, was damaged by Fulke Fitz Warine *c.*1203 and again by the Welsh in 1212. The castle seems to have been abandoned by the le Stranges soon afterwards in favour of the more open site at Knockin (q.v.) and was ruinous by 1272. Purchased from the le Strange family by the Earl of Arundel in 1302, it was rebuilt by 1313 before passing to Roger Mortimer, Earl of March, in 1326. It reverted to the Earl of Arundel in 1330 following Mortimer's execution by Edward III but seems to have been permanently abandoned in the 1360s, the last reference to it being in 1364. Its stone is known to have been removed to repair the nearby church tower.

The surviving fragments stand on a low platform which may represent the original motte and presumably date from the rebuilding of the castle in the

112 The fragmentary remains of the keep at Ruyton-XI-Towns, now surrounded by the graveyard of the nearby church, which stands to the right just out of shot in this photo

early fourteenth century. What remains are the defaced rubble fragments of the north, south and west walls of a keep, originally about 14m square, which have been almost entirely robbed of their ashlar facings. The fragments are some 3m thick, standing to a height of up to 4m and bear the damaged traces of window shafts in the south and west walls. They stand only a few metres west of the twelfth-century church of St John the Baptist.

Ryton Motte SJ 761029

The eroded remains of a motte stand in the gardens of a house approximately 125m north of the church in Ryton, overlooking the valley of the River Worfe. The mound has a summit diameter of approximately 7.5m with faint traces of a ditch to its south-east. Excavation revealed this to have been approximately 3m deep and up to 5m wide and it is possible that its bailey lay to the east. Nothing is known of the castle's history, though in 1086 the manor was held of Earl Roger by Osbern, son of Richard Scrope (of Richard's Castle). It descended in the Fitz Alan family.

Sandford Mound SJ 581344

The small steep-sided mound in the grounds north of Sandford Hall is of uncertain origin. Long regarded as a castle mound, it has also been considered to be a garden feature or gazebo base and occurs as such in a map of 1775. Of course, its later use as a garden feature does not preclude an origin as a motte. The mound has a base diameter of approximately 25m, around 7m across the summit, and stands over 5m high. It is said to have been surrounded by a shallow ditch. If it was a motte, it could only have supported a small structure like a watch tower and now carries a water-tower, the successor to a small reservoir built in the 1920s.

Shrawardine Castle SJ 401184 ★★

In 1086, Shrawardine was one of the extensive holdings of Reginald (Rainald) de Bailleul, Sheriff of Shropshire, who may have built the original motte and bailey in the village. A more substantial castle was probably constructed during the reign of Henry I (1100-35) though the first reference to it does not occur until 1165, when Philip Helgot acknowledged his feudal duty of 'castle guard' – a period of garrison duty – which had been rendered by his predecessors. Henry II spent considerable sums on repairs to Shrawardine but it was destroyed by the Welsh in 1215. Henry III gave Shrawardine to John Fitz Alan who rebuilt the castle (*c.*1220-40); it became an important centre of the Fitz Alan barony and received the service of 'castle guard' from a number of their tenants. The rebuilt castle was known as 'Castle Isabel' in honour of John Fitz Alan's wife. The Fitz Alans remained in occupation until 1583 when the castle was sold to the Lord Chancellor, Sir Thomas Bromley, and his family, represented by Henry Bromley, was in occupation during the Civil War.

Henry Bromley was captured at the fall of Shrewsbury in February 1645 but Shrawardine was held for the king by Sir Richard Vaughan. He wrought such destruction on the village – demolishing many of its houses and even the church to clear fields of fire and supply materials to strengthen the castle – that he earned the nickname 'the Devil of Shrawardine'. However, despite these measures the castle held out for only five days when attacked by Parliamentary forces in June 1645, during Sir Richard's temporary absence, and the garrison was allowed to march to Ludlow. To prevent its reoccupation, Parliament ordered the demolition of the castle, much of the stone being carried to Shrewsbury to repair its castle and town walls.

113 The main castle mound at Shrawardine from the north-east, with the few fragments of its masonry structure

114 The sole remains of the fine sandstone wall which once encased the mound at Shrawardine. The outlet of a garderobe chute is visible to the right

The site lies on a rise overlooking the Severn, with Little Shrawardine (q.v.) only 800m away on the opposite bank, and commands the valley route and river crossing. The motte is 50 x 30m in area, standing to a height of up to 5m, and bears the remains of a shell keep which actually surrounded the motte. The only substantial fragments of its walls lie on the western face of the mound and comprise several courses of dressed sandstone, with a distinct batter, the remains of three blind arches and the outlet of a garderobe chute. Only a few pieces of stonework remain on the summit of the motte, one of which may be a gateway tower, one of two round towers which defended the main entrance to the castle at the south-east of the motte. The uneven ground on the summit undoubtedly marks the location of masonry fragments and the foundations of buildings. The quality of the existing stonework, little as there is, implies that Shrawardine was a strong and imposing castle.

The main bailey, some 90 x 50m, lay to the north of the castle and is defined to its east and west by what are now very low banks and the faintest traces of a ditch. The most substantial remains of the bailey defences – a section of a bank and deep ditch – lie east of the motte. The bailey opens into another, smaller rectangular enclosure to its south, immediately west of the mound, which is bounded along the road to its west by a ditch which is clearly visible for part of its course. What appear to be building platforms within this enclosure may represent the location of village houses destroyed in 1645; the present village and the church lie to the south of the castle. Other medieval ditches and banks, presumed to have been associated with the castle defences, have been revealed by excavation.

Shrewsbury Castle SJ 388206 ★★★

Shrewsbury, Shropshire's county town, stands in a fine defensive position almost entirely surrounded by a loop of the Severn. The only landward approach is a by narrow neck of land to the north and it is likely that this was defended by Saxon earthworks. Because of the natural strength of the site, a large castle was never necessary and Shrewsbury does not bear comparison in size with other great border fortresses like Ludlow or Chepstow, or Edward I's castles at Conwy or Caernarfon. Nevertheless, the castle, the town walls and the fortified bridges across the Severn created a strong defensive unit.

The strength and strategic significance of the site were not lost on the Normans and as early as 1067 William I ordered the construction of a castle in the town. There was certainly a royal fortress of some kind by 1069 when it was unsuccessfully attacked by the Welsh and Edric 'the Wild'. Around 1071, Roger of Montgomery was created Palatine Earl of Shrewsbury and began the construction of a major motte and bailey to serve as an administrative centre and military base. Domesday Book records that the sites of 51 houses were taken up by the building of the castle and whilst this might have been a military necessity, it represents a massive incursion into a small town.

After the rebellion of 1102 and the abolition of the Earldom of Shrewsbury, the castle reverted to the Crown. Seized by William Fitz Alan, it was held for Queen Matilda against King Stephen during their civil war and successfully besieged by Stephen in 1138. It is reported that he hanged 100 of the garrison from the walls. In the 1150s, reconstruction in stone began, with the inner bailey's timber walls replaced by sandstone and heavy expenditure recorded in the royal records between 1164-1224. Traces of this work may survive in the lower parts of the bailey wall (with its short, straight, angular stretches) and the lower

Above: 115 The large tree-covered motte at Shrewsbury, with Laura's Tower (right)

Left: 116 The postern gate in the east wall at Shrewsbury. A seventeenth-century refurbishment of a medieval original, which once gave access to the river frontage of the castle

117 The West Tower and part of the hall block at Shrewsbury. Prior to the raising of the hall's height in the late sixteenth century, the end towers would have stood out rather more than they now do

floor of the hall block. Attacks by the Welsh, who burned the town in 1215 and 1234, prompted the construction of town walls, completed *c.*1250. These mainly followed the high ground within the loop of the Severn, connecting its two fortified bridges, and joined the castle on its western side. Traces of the walls are still to be seen – most clearly on 'Town Walls' and behind shop buildings on the lower slopes of Pride Hill – but only one tower remains. This small, square structure dating to the fourteenth century and later restored, stands on Town Walls. Nothing remains of the town's gates or fortified bridges.

Earl Roger's original castle comprised a large mound, much of which still exists, with a small inner bailey, 82 x 45m, now enclosed by later sandstone walls and a larger outer bailey which stretched westwards into the town. The evidence suggests that this had only earth and timber defences with ditches, though there may have been partial reconstruction in stone under Henry II. This bailey was being encroached upon by the mid-thirteenth century and by the late fourteenth century, or earlier, had been built over.

Its location on the Welsh frontier gave Shrewsbury Castle a leading role in the border conflicts of the thirteenth century and it was a major base for operations against the Welsh under Edward I, who was at Shrewsbury in 1277 and 1282. However, although the completed castle is often cited as Edward's creation, royal building records show that most expenditure on new building was made by Henry III (1216-72) and included the hall and towers, barbican defences and a drawbridge. Recent work in tree-ring dating also supports building in the mid-thirteenth century. Under Edward I (1272-1306) comparatively small sums were spent, presumably on minor alterations or the completion of existing projects and not on major new work.

After the conquest of Wales, Shrewsbury Castle went into a rapid decline and, despite its royal status and location in the county town, does not seem to have been kept in repair. It was in a poor state as early as 1336 and is recorded as 'wasted' in 1420. A survey in 1443 reported that all its 'howsing' (presumably its internal buildings) had collapsed and that only the weakened walls were left. Although repairs were effected in 1451-3, by the time of Leland's survey in the 1540s the castle was 'muche in ruine'. The so-called 'Burghley Map', dated to *c.*1575 but possibly earlier, shows the inner bailey buildings in ruin and the hall as a two-storeyed, roofless structure.

The castle's resurrection began in 1565 when it was leased by Elizabeth I to a wealthy local merchant, Richard Onslow. During his 30-year tenure, he began the conversion of the ruined fortress into a town house. Onslow added the hall's third storey, with its distinctive square, mullioned windows, and probably re-roofed the hall using the massive wooden beams which still exist. Apart from the brief refortification during the Civil Wars, Shrewsbury Castle remained as a large town house for the next 300 years.

The castle was granted to the town in 1596 and further restoration was carried out, especially to the bailey walls. In 1642, Shrewsbury declared for the king, who was entertained in the town in that year – though he stayed in the nearby Council House, not in the castle. The castle and town walls were hurriedly repaired under the king's Lieutenant General in Shropshire, lord Capel and by his successor, Prince Rupert. The iron-studded oak gates to the inner bailey were set up in 1643, as were the gates on the postern, which may have been repaired at the same time. The former still bear the marks of musket balls to their outer surfaces, though from what date is uncertain. A sandstone barbican or gateway defence was built outside the main gates, with musket-slits covering the immediate approach to the doors. It was presumably a form of roofed blockhouse, though only its inner walls remain. Despite these expensive repairs, the castle's military career was brief and inglorious. In February 1645, Parliamentary forces from Wem under the German mercenary, Colonel Reinking, laid siege to the castle. By then, additional defences in the form of ditches, palisades and earth banks had been thrown up to the north of the castle and along its river front. However, Parliamentary forces found a gap in the palisade along the river and by what was probably an act of treachery gained entrance to the town through St Mary's Water Gate. A fight in The Square led to the town's rapid surrender, leaving the castle in a dangerous plight. The garrison chose the safer option of surrender and was allowed to march to Ludlow. Shrewsbury's fall was a major blow to the royal cause on the Welsh border and to Royalist morale. The castle was garrisoned throughout the rest of the Civil War and repaired using (amongst others) materials from Shrawardine Castle but although briefly involved in abortive Royalist uprisings in 1655 and 1659, it saw no further military action.

In 1663, the town surrendered the castle to Charles II, who gave it to Sir Francis Newport, later Earl of Bradford. It thus reverted in the late seventeenth century to the role of town house and passed through a number of tenants until acquired *c*.1780 by Sir William Pulteney, MP for Shrewsbury after 1775 and reputedly the wealthiest commoner in England. He began a wholesale reconstruction, employing the young Thomas Telford who was then County Surveyor. Much that is now visible is the work of this reconstruction, including most of the battlements, 'Laura's Tower', the main doorway on the lower floor and the large windows piercing the walls of the west tower and hall. Internally, two rooms in the West Tower, the Mayor's Parlour and the Circular Room, retain the plasterwork decoration from this era. Otherwise, little is known about the internal division of the space. Occupied until 1910, the castle was purchased in 1924 by the Shropshire Horticultural Society and presented to the town. For most of the twentieth century, the hall was used as the Borough Council chamber but when larger premises were needed in the 1970s, the castle became empty. Since 1985, it has been the home of the Shropshire Regimental Museum.

The man-made motte is an impressive structure, although now smaller in extent than it originally was, with a base diameter of 60 x 73m. It stands to a height of about 13m from the inner bailey but is much more impressive viewed from the south, where it sweeps down over 30m to the Severn. It was originally dominated by a large wooden keep or *donjon* over 12m high, probably a complex structure of several storeys; it was surrounded until after 1266 by a wooden palisade. Sometime later, after the tower collapsed *c.*1270, a weak sandstone wall was built around the summit, its footings still visible beneath the later wall which now exists. Between 1269-71 the motte was undercut by the Severn and slumped into the river, taking the wooden keep with it. This necessitated the construction of a new retaining wall, in fine Grinshill stone, on the south-east face of the remaining motte, creating an elongated D-shaped summit with an area of approximately 30.5 x 15m. The keep was replaced by a small watchtower at the south-west angle of the motte — perhaps the motte was not deemed strong enough to support anything larger. This simple round tower, shown in eighteenth-century prints, was replaced in 1790 by the present 'Laura's Tower', a two-storey gazebo reputedly built as a birthday gift for his daughter by Sir William Pulteney. It stands on the base of the earlier tower, which is clearly visible (*colour plate 25*).

The hall extends to 28 x 7m, with walls over 2m thick on the north side and about 1.5m thick on the south, where it faced the inner bailey. It has three floors — the lowest dated to the mid-twelfth century, the central level to the mid-thirteenth century and the upper level to Onslow's restoration in the late sixteenth century. The massive wooden ceiling is probably Onslow's addition, though it may have been completed in the early seventeenth century by the town council. The great windows which pierce the north and south walls of the second floor were inserted by Telford during Sir William Pulteney's restoration in the 1790s, as were the large windows in the West Tower (*colour plate 31*).

The West and East towers, often claimed to be Edwardian, are likely to date to *c.*1250 in the reign of Henry III. Before the raising of the hall in the late sixteenth century, they would have stood much higher above the block than they now do — as seen in the Burghley Map of *c.*1575. Their sandstone walls are on average 1.8m thick, with the windows a variety of types adapted or inserted over generations and varying from original narrow slits (as in the East Tower) to the large 'Gothick' windows inserted by Telford. The West Tower has three floors — a windowless lower basement, a middle room now used as the Mayor's Parlour and retaining its late eighteeenth-century deco-ration and with 'Gothick' windows piercing its walls, and an upper room now used as a store. Fragments in this room, including a thirteenth-century corbel and the remains of stone ribs, show that it originally had a vaulted ceiling. The East Tower equally has a windowless storeroom at its base, a central room and an upper storey, now used as museum offices and display areas. It should be borne in mind that the castle, being in a large town, was probably never intended to be a grand residence in its earlier days – the town itself would have provided accommodation for important visitors and their retinues.

The hall was originally entered at its modern level – a raised doorway on the east side of the middle floor – though the present entrance is a modern restoration. The large doorway piercing the south wall of the lower floor was inserted by Telford and was the main entrance to the building from the 1790s. The great fireplace on the middle floor is in its original location, though heavily restored, and the 'minstrels' galleries' at the west and east end of the hall are modern additions, created when the upper floor was removed in the early twentieth century. The location of service rooms like the kitchen is not known; originally, they may have been in separate buildings in the inner bailey. The stone-lined well in the inner bailey sinks to a depth of 22m and there may have been another – sometimes called 'the siege well' – under the floor in the 'Circular Room' at the base of the West Tower.

The postern gate in the east wall originally gave access to the river frontage of the castle, but this side was dug away during the building of the railway station in the 1840s. The battlemented tower, with an upper room approximately 6 x 4.5m, with plain mullioned windows, dates from the seventeenth century, possibly restored at the beginning of the Civil War. However, it must replace an earlier gateway, perhaps thirteenth century, and retains a blocked portcullis groove. Its heavy wooden doorways presumably date, like the main gates, to the strengthening of the castle's defences at the outset of the Civil War.

The inner bailey is surrounded by sandstone walls of various ages and the product of numerous restorations. They stand up to 8m in height and are from only 0.75-1.5m thick. The bailey is entered by a twelfth-century archway, 2.7m wide. It looks decidedly weak as a main gateway – there is no trace of a tower or portcullis (which even the postern gate had) though there must have been a ditch crossed by a drawbridge beyond the gate. It is possible that the gateway has been extensively altered and its wooden doors and barbican certainly date to the refortification at the outset of the Civil War. The battlements on the west section of the wall may date from the Civil War period, but most of the rest are creations of Telford's restoration and later. A doorway from the East Tower staircase led onto a wall-walk on that side and there is a wall-work on the western stretch of wall and to the south of the main gate. The small 'sally port' in the west wall may date to the early seventeenth-century refurbishment.

The buildings of the bailey, which might have included stables and barns etc. have gone, though a recent geophysical survey has revealed evidence of their location. The largest structure was the chapel of St Michael, mentioned in Domesday but in ruins by the late fourteenth century. In the outer bailey stood the late twelfth-century chapel of St Nicholas. This became the chapel of the nearby Council House, used by the Council of Wales when on circuit in Shrewsbury. It gradually fell into ruin and its remnants were demolished in the mid-nineteenth century to allow for the construction of the now-redundant church of St Nicholas. It is believed that the archway set alongside the castle's main gate was the original chancel arch of this church, re-used as a decorative feature in a nineteenth-century restoration.

Sibdon Carwood Castle so 435818

The attractive two-storey mansion near the church at Sibdon Carwood stands on or near the site an earlier castle which Leland called 'Shepton Corbet'

118 Sibdon Carwood: an attractive country house, but with no trace of an earlier castle

of which nothing remains. The house was built by the Corbets early in the seventeenth century and remodelled by their successors, the Walcots, and by the Fleming family in the eighteenth century. Further alterations to give the house a castellated appearance were undertaken by the Holdens early in the nineteenth century.

Smethcott Motte SO 448994

The ancient settlement of Smethcott is now reduced to a few scattered houses and its church but in Domesday Book, the manor was held of Earl Roger by Edmund and from him by Aldred, its previous tenant. Smethcott became part of the Honour of Montgomery but the castle is presumed to have been abandoned *c.*1270-72 when the manor passed to the Burnell family of Acton Burnell.

The motte stands in 'Castle Field', only metres from the west door of the Norman church of St Michael, on an east–west ridge above a steep-sided valley to the south. The flattened mound now rises to only 2.5-3m, with a base diameter of about 40m. It was very much eroded by ploughing and deliberately reduced to provide soil and rubble for road building in the eighteenth century. The bailey, which is approximately 50 x 35m across, lay to the south of the motte but only faint traces of its perimeter banks remain.

119 The low castle mound at Smethcott (skyline, centre) and the nearby church of St Michael (left)

Excavations in the 1950s indicated occupation in the late twelfth and thirteenth centuries, with timber structures on the summit of the motte and stonework fragments nearby. Although there are no visible traces, the excavations revealed a V-shaped ditch around the base of the motte and that of the bailey probably survives as a buried feature.

Soulton Castle SJ 546303

Soulton was held of Earl Roger by the church of St Michael, which was the chapel of Shrewsbury Castle and presumably founded by Earl Roger himself. It later passed into the tenancy of Robert Corbet and was held from him by the *de Suleton* family in the twelfth century.

The castle, probably built by the de Suletons, lies along the present B5065, immediately north-east of the fine Caroline Soulton Hall, built *c.*1680 by the Hill family. The rectangular mound, effectively a small island within a wide moat, stands less than 3m high and measures approximately 20 x 16m across its summit. The moat is well-defined, especially to the north and west, where it is up to 15m wide and 2m deep. The eastern side of the site lies alongside, and was presumably defended by, the Soulton Brook but the ditch and bank on the south have been largely destroyed by the construction of the road. The entrance to the site lay at the south-west and there are slight traces of

120 The mound at Soulton with traces of its surrounding moat and outer banks

platforms on the mound which presumably represent its internal buildings and defences. The site may have been incorporated into the formal gardens of Soulton Hall during the post-medieval period.

Stapleton Motte SJ 472044 ★

The large motte at Stapleton 'in Legharness' is another which stands very close to an early church. In this case, half of the mound actually lies in the graveyard of the church of St John the Baptist, only 50m to its south-east. The attractive church may date to as early as 1190-1210, but was extensively remodelled *c.*1790 and 1840-70.

Stapleton was held by Alward in 1086 and then descended in the Honour of Montgomery to the Cantilupes and other families. The castle was probably built in the early twelfth century and was in the hands of King John by 1207. Later in the thirteenth century, the manor passed to the Stapleton family, who provided Sheriffs of Shropshire in the late thirteenth and fourteenth centuries. They presumably built the formerly moated manor house, Moat Farm, which lies south-west of the village and which may have replaced the castle as a principal residence in the fourteenth century.

The mound rises to over 3.5m, with a level summit about 20m across. It stands on ground sloping southwards towards a tributary of the Cound Brook and commanded a nearby ford, which is still in use. It would also have controlled a section of the valley route running south of Shrewsbury. Part of

121 The tree-covered motte at Stapleton near the church of St John

the summit of the motte lies within the graveyard and has graves dug into it. There is little trace of any surrounding ditch and no signs of a bailey, which presumably lay in the area occupied by the church.

Stoke-upon-Tern Castle SJ 646276

Hardly anything remains of the castle or moated house which stood about 250m south-south-east of the present Stoke manor in Stoke-upon-Tern. In 1086 the manor was held of Earl Roger by Roger de Lacy and was some-times known as Stoke Lacy. By the thirteenth century its subtenants were the de Say family and it was exchanged by them *c.*1250 for land held by the Verdon (de Verdun) family who retained ownership into the fourteenth cen-tury. After a complicated descent through various hands, the manor passed to the Corbets of Adderley in the early fifteenth century.

122 Plan of the site at Stoke-upon-Tern. Very little now remains to be seen on the ground

Little is known of the history of the castle. By 1629, whatever was on the site – fortress or house – was owned by Sir John Corbet and was garrisoned for the King during the Civil War. It fell to Parliamentary forces in 1644 and seems to have been slighted during the war or completely demolished just afterwards; a conveyance of 1668 refers only to stone and other materials 'on the place where the castle had lately stood'.

During drainage work at various times, large blocks of sandstone, seventeenth-century brickwork, limestone roofing slabs and other building materials have been found. But the site has suffered greatly from generations of ploughing and all that remains visible is the slightly raised rectangular building platform surrounded by the traces of a moat and bank. The enclosure measures approximately 80 x 50m, with parts of the moat and bank visible to the north-east and west.

Stokesay Castle SO 436817 ★★★

Stokesay Castle is one of the most familiar castle sites in Shropshire. It is usual to call it a fortified manor house and underplay its strength as a 'castle' but whilst its surviving curtain walls are weak and its gatehouse purely decorative, some elements – especially the south tower – are fairly formidable and, additionally, defended by a wide water-filled moat, it may have been rather more secure than its present state suggests.

In 1086 the manor was held of Earl Roger by Roger de Lacy and became part of the de Lacy Liberty of Stanton Long. A branch of the de Says of Clun were tenants of the de Lacy's before 1115 when the manor was held by Theodoric de Say. From them 'Stoke' took its suffix, which survived despite the fact that the family connection ceased in the 1250s. The de Says built their first residence on the site *c.*1200 and added the north tower *c.*1240. In the mid-thirteenth century, the castle passed to John de Verdun and around 1281 to the wealthy local wool merchant Lawrence de Ludlow. He completely restructured the castle between 1281-1295 so that most of what remains dates from one period of construction. Granted licence to crenellate in 1291, de Ludlow is believed to have built the hall and solar block, the south tower, the wooden storey on the north tower and the original curtain wall. Most of the fabric would therefore date to much the same time as Acton Burnell (q.v.) though they are very different – one a provincial fortified house and the

123 An aerial view of the fortified manor house at Stokesay. *CPAT-93-C-577*

other the stylish residence of an important officer of state. De Ludlow died in 1296 but Stokesay remained in the family until 1497, when it passed by marriage to the Vernons of Tong and in the 1590s was sold to the Mainwarings. Purchased by the Craven family in 1620, the attractive half-timbered gatehouse is thought to have been built about that time by its tenant Sir Charles Baldwin, whose family lived at Stokesay until the early eighteenth century. Saxton's map of 1577 shows a park west and south of Stokesay church and seventeenth-century maps (e.g. those of Speed in 1611 and Morden in 1695) indicate that the park embraced the castle.

Occupied by Sir Charles Baldwin at the outset of the Civil War and garrisoned for the king under a Captain Daurett as an important stronghold on the Shrewsbury–Ludlow road, Stokesay remained untroubled until 1645. Parliamentary forces under Colonel Reinking arrived to besiege the castle early in June 1645, but after negotiations its garrison simply surrendered and an immediate Royalist response, in the form of an army sent to retake Stokesay on 8 June, was defeated at Wistanstow. The castle remained in Parliamentary hands and although the curtain walls were demolished upon Parliament's order after the war, Stokesay escaped lightly with no other slighting imposed.

124 The seventeenth-century gatehouse at Stokesay: a purely decorative entrance probably on the site of an earlier, fortified gate

The castle was repaired by Sir Samuel Baldwin (d.1683) after the Restoration but does not seem to have been in permanent occupation as a country house much after 1680 and most of his new building was removed in the early nineteenth century. From *c*.1728 Stokesay was leased out as a farm but by the early nineteenth century was in a state of ruin, with only parts of it in use as workshops and stores. Consolidation began in the mid-nineteenth century by lord Craven and restoration continued in the late nineteenth century by J.D. Allcroft, who bought the castle in 1869. Although still in private ownership, Stokesay Castle has been administered by English Heritage since the 1990s.

The castle stands on the west bank of the River Onny, 1km south of Craven Arms. Its irregular courtyard extends to approximately 44 x 37m, enclosed by a stone curtain wall which originally stood to over 10m and carried a wall-walk. The present wall, much lower and of no great strength, is largely a restoration of the defences slighted in 1647, though a portion stands to its original height at the east corner of the south tower. The castle is surrounded by an impressive moat, between 4-6m wide and 2m deep. Once water-filled, it was supplied by the pool lying to its west (*colour plate 15*). The castle is entered via a decorative half-timbered gatehouse. Clearly not a defensive structure, it presumably occupies the site of an earlier, stronger gateway; it has been dated to the 1620s or later, to the post Civil War restoration. The internal buildings which would have cluttered the small courtyard – such as the kitchen, which lay near the north tower and was standing until 1814 – have gone and only the well remains.

The polygonal north tower may be as early as *c*.1240 and has walls slightly less than 1m thick. Over a basement cellar, it contains apartments and bed-rooms and a fine fireplace of *c*.1300 in the second floor room. Its most interesting structure is the projecting wooden storey on top of the tower.

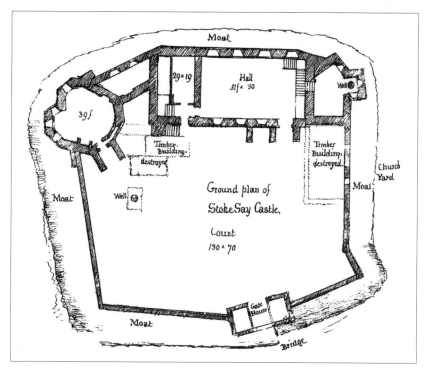

125 A late Victorian plan of the castle at Stokesay, with the location of vanished buildings indicated

Dated to *c.*1290-1300, this rare feature may be an important survival, perhaps hinting that other stone castles carried wooden-framed structures (now gone) on their upper levels.

The most significant defensive feature is the polygonal south tower, built *c.*1280-95 (*colour plate 19*). Perhaps associated with the licence to crenellate in 1291, it is a much more formidable structure than any other on the site and was originally entered (as was common with such towers) on its first floor. Standing to over 20m high, with walls nearly 2m thick, it was not accessible from any other building and could have stood as an independent 'citadel' in case of attack. Two projecting faces overlook and defend the curtain wall to the south. Inside, it houses a cellar and two storeys of rooms – probably bedrooms – accessed from a staircase built into the thickness of the wall. It has only single lancet windows, in keeping with its defensive function, and is topped with original battlements with cross-loops and a small turret. The flat roof is modern, replacing a low-pitched, tiled roof which existed until 1868.

Between the towers is a domestic block with a fine example of a medieval open hall. It is approximately 12m at its highest, 10m wide and over 17m long. Probably built by Lawrence de Ludlow between 1280-95, it may stand on

126 The hall block at Stokesay from the courtyard

the site of an earlier wooden structure contemporary with the north tower (*c.*1240). Although altered in the nineteenth century (e.g. with the outer buttresses added *c.*1866), it retains many original features. The hall has four bays, each with its own gable, lit by tall, decorated windows typical of the late thirteenth century, with integral seats set deeply into the wall. The hall was heated only by a central hearth, whose smoke would have been directed through a simple opening in the roof. The roof timbers have been dated to various periods, some being original, with alterations in the fifteenth century and possibly in the nineteenth. Steps connect the hall directly to the basement of the north tower but the tower's upper floors can be reached only by an open wooden staircase.

The south end of the hall block comprises the solar or lord's private apartments and dates mainly from the 1280s, though its cellar and undercroft may be earlier. Above the cellar was a living room (at hall level) and the lord's private apartment or solar above that. The solar, some 10 x 6m, was accessed only by an external staircase, originally wooden (the present staircase being more recent) but reflects the fact that Stokesay was becoming more a comfortable residence than a fortification by the end of the thirteenth century as the Welsh frontier became more peaceful. In the seventeenth century, a fine carved Flemish overmantel was set into the medieval chimney breast of this apartment, which at the time was used as a dining room by the Baldwins. The solar and hall is connected to the south tower by a small block with two rooms, the lower dated to *c.*1300 and the upper to *c.*1650; they may have been used as servants' quarters or stores.

Sundorne Castle SJ 518152

Sundorne Castle, 5.5km north-east of Shrewsbury, is the only castle in this gazetteer to have no medieval foundation as such. The first house was simply a grange of nearby Haughmond Abbey, purchased by the Hill family after the Dissolution. The site passed to the Corbets in 1638 and the first mansion was erected *c.*1730. Around 1800, this was remodelled as a red-brick 'castle' for John Corbet, possibly by George Wyatt. It overlooked a huge artificial lake, Sundorne Pool, of which only a silted portion remains, and incorporated towers, battlements, castellated garden walls, a large 'medieval' gatehouse and its own 'Gothick' chapel. The estates associated with the house – mostly

127 The remains of the castellated mansion at Sundorne near Shrewsbury: the Chapel (left) looking towards the gatehouse. Behind this row stand stables and farm buildings, now dilpidated

former lands of Haughmond Abbey – were very extensive and included Haughmond Hill, on which the Corbets built the sham 'Haughmond Castle' as a hunting lodge, *c.*1770. It no longer remains, having collapsed in 1931.

The Corbets moved out of the castle in 1894 and it passed through various tenants until the end of the First World War. In common with other large country houses, it was found impossible to maintain in the post-war world and its lands were gradually sold off. Left empty for years, the mansion fell into decay and in September 1955 it was demolished – despite its status as a scheduled monument of accepted architectural merit. However a considerable amount still survives in the form of the farm, the walled kitchen garden, the gatehouse, the chapel and the castellated remains of the outbuildings (now dilapidated). They are an attractive reminder of what was a fine country house right on the outskirts of the county town.

Tong Motte and Castle SJ 292069

In 1086, the manor of Tong was directly held by Earl Roger, having been owned by the Saxon Earl Morcar. Roger gave Tong church to Shrewsbury Abbey but soon after the forfeiture of the estates of Robert of Bellême in 1102, the manor was granted to Richard de Belmeis, Bishop of London (d.1127). Later in the century, it came into the hands of the La Zouche family who held Tong until *c.*1250, when the manor passed by marriage to William Harcourt and thence to the de Pembridge family.

Castle Mound at Tong Norton ★

Half a kilometre north of Tong church lie the remains of a large motte. Shaped out of a natural sandstone knoll, it stands east of the crossroads at Tong Norton. The mound is up to 5m high, with a summit diameter of 32 x 28m and has clear traces of its surrounding ditch on the southern side. It lies in marshy ground by the junction of the River Wolfe with another stream, but from a defensive point of view is somewhat overlooked by higher ground nearby. To the south of the mound lay a roughly triangular bailey, defined on its eastern side by a bank slightly less than 1m high.

128 The castle mound at Tong Norton

A castle at Tong – presumably this one – is referred to in 1098 and it may be the 'olde castle' mentioned in a Pembridge document of 1320. Nothing is known of its history, but it presumably fell into disuse on the construction of the castle to its south (see below).

Tong Castle

A new castle, presumably of earth and timber, was constructed about 1km south of the old motte, probably by Richard de Belmeis, Bishop of London. He was granted the manor by Henry I after its forfeiture following Robert of Bellême's rebellion in 1102. Thereafter it has a complicated history of ownership and reconstruction. Under the Zouche family in the late twelfth century, its bailey was walled with stone and shortly afterwards an outer bailey was added to the north. The footings of the inner bailey towers and gatehouse were discovered during excavations prior to the construction of the M54 motorway. The castle was owned by the Harcourts in the mid-thirteenth century and a 'park' is recorded in 1273. At the end of the century, it passed to the Pembridge family and Fulk Pembridge IV is believed to have reduced whatever was there for the construction of a new manor house, lying on a north–south axis between the old inner and outer baileys. Licence to crenellate was granted by Richard II in 1381-2. In 1447 Tong castle passed to the Vernons of Haddon Hall, whose family tombs are one of the treasures of the nearby church. It was

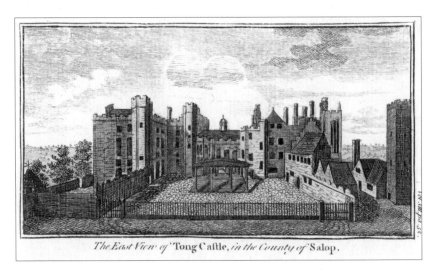

The East View of Tong Castle, *in the County of* Salop.

129 The Vernon mansion at Tong from a print of *c.*1760

largely rebuilt as a brick mansion by Sir Henry Vernon *c.*1500-15; the Saxton map of 1577 shows the castle, with a park lying to its east.

Tong was one of comparatively few castles in Shropshire which declared for Parliament on the outbreak of the Civil War. Then owned by William Pierrepoint, formerly MP for Much Wenlock, and an opponent of Charles I, it was seized for the king by Francis Ottley in 1643. Taken by Parliamentary forces from Eccleshall in December, it was recaptured by the Royalists under Prince Rupert in April 1644 after a fortnight's siege, but with the collapse of the royal cause Tong appears to have been slighted or partially damaged. A reference in 1763 relates that the east wing had been demolished in the Civil War and then rebuilt in brick, to match the rest of the house.

The mansion continued in occupation into the early eighteenth century but by the 1730s seems to have been neglected. A watercolour by N. Buck shows the Vernon castle around that time, in the final years of its existence. It was sold in 1760 to George Durant the Elder (d.1780), an eccentric with a passion for architecture who commissioned 'Capability' Brown to reconstruct the house (1764-65) in an elaborate and fantastical style mixing the Gothick with the 'Moorish'.

The 'castle' remained in occupation until just before the First World War, a strikingly original sight in the Shropshire countryside. Most of it was dismantled in 1913 and what was left of its shell was demolished as unsafe by lord Newport in 1954. The construction of the M54 motorway through the site in the 1970s destroyed most of what was left. A few fragments of a kitchen, a possible chapel and other features are visible immediately to the south of the M54, just west of Junction 3, in what was the inner bailey of the original castle. Remnants of a stable block survive on the north side of the motorway in what is a fraction of the old outer bailey.

Toot Hill SO 682760 *

Just east of Cleobury Mortimer, standing on a height above the River Rea, is the earthwork known as Castle Toot or Toot Hill. It was clearly intended to control the valley and the crossing of the Rea and may have begun life as an Iron Age promontory fort. The castle comprises a semicircular enclosure roughly 61 x 28m, carved out of a spur of land overlooking the valley. It is defended by an impressive ditch and outer bank on all sides except the

130 Part of the high platform and deep ditch at Castle Toot

north-west, where the fall of land towards the Rea obviates the need for additional defences. The site was entered on its north-eastern side, where traces of a gateway and bridge across the ditch have been found. Other pieces of masonry were visible into the eighteenth century and have occasionally been found in building work on the site, implying that a stone castle existed there at some stage. A large house was built in the centre of the enclosure in the 1950s.

Unless Toot Hill is actually the castle referred to in twelfth-century accounts of Cleobury Mortimer (q.v.), nothing is known of its history.

Tyrley Castle SJ 678330

In 1086, Tyrley, then a Staffordshire manor, was held of Earl Roger by William Pantulf. The castle, presumably built by the Pantulfs of Wem, was well sited on a north-facing ridge with sheer slopes down to the Tern, just south of Market Drayton. Tyrley probably began life as an earth and timber castle which was rebuilt in stone, possibly by Ralph le Boteler (Butler), when the manor passed

131 The eighteenth-century brick farmhouse at Tyrley near Market Drayton, probably standing on the site of the earlier castle

into Butler hands in the thirteenth century. The keep may have stood on the rocky outcrop where the farm now stands, but evidence suggests that the stone castle was never completed and that Tyrley became a manor house rather than a fortification. The name 'Tyrley Castle' occurs in the late sixteenth century when the house was owned by Sir William Gerard and may be a deliberate revival of the old name of the site.

Excavations in the 1880s and in 1910 revealed lengths of stone walling and the existence of a wide ditch but nothing now remains of the castle, whose site is occupied by Tyrley Castle Farm. This is a late eighteenth-century brick farmhouse, although sandstone blocks in the farm buildings may be re-used stone from the castle. Fragmentary earthworks around the site are thought to relate to garden landscaping rather than earlier defences. The bailey may have stood in the area occupied by the present farm buildings, just to the east of the farmhouse.

132 The distinctive motte at Gwarthlow, recently cleared of its covering of trees

Upper Gwarthlow Motte so 252955 ★

From the south, the motte 400m north-east of Upper Gwarthlow Farm stands out starkly against the surrounding landscape, especially since it has recently been cleared of its covering of trees. Rising to a height of about 6m, the motte is cut out of a hill standing on a slight ridge, allowing excellent views in all directions. It has a base diameter of approximately 28m and its oval summit extends to approximately 13 x 11m. Traces of the surrounding ditch are only visible on the eastern side of the mound and there is no clear trace of a bailey.

It is assumed that the castle represents the *caput* or principal seat of the manor of Rhiston. In 1086, this was one of a number of estates held of Earl Roger by Alward, 'son of Almund' and became part of the Honour of Montgomery. Nothing is known of its history.

Warfield Bank Ringwork so 371774 ★

A well-defined ringwork lies on the slopes of Warfield Bank, south-east of Hopton. As with the ringwork at Cheney Longville (q.v.), local tradition

133 The earthwork at Warfield, near Hopton

regards the site as a Civil War gun emplacement whose target would have been Hopton Castle (q.v.), which is clearly visible 600m to the north-west.

The isolated knoll was carefully chosen as a strong defensive position and has excellent views in all directions. Its circular rampart, up to 2m high and 6-8m wide, has an overall diameter of 40m, protecting an inner area of approximately 25m. The surrounding ditch has mostly been filled in or ploughed away, but is visible to the west and south-east. What may be the original entrance pierces the rampart to the north-north-east.

The interior would have been level with the land outside, but quarrying for the stone which lies near the surface has disturbed the ground. A water-filled hollow in the centre of the site may be result of this digging rather than an original feature; a small quarry lies only a few metres downhill to the north-east.

Wattlesborough Castle SJ 355126 ★★

Wattlesborough, held of Earl Roger by Roger Fitz Corbet in 1086, descended as part of the Corbet Barony of Caus and passed in the twelfth century to the branch of the family which built Moreton Corbet. In the 1380s it was granted to the la Pole family and in the late fifteenth century to the Leightons. Wattlesborough remained their principal residence until the family moved to a refurbished mansion on their estate at Loton Park in 1712 and it is believed that stonework from the castle was taken for use on the new house and for alterations to Alberbury church.

Wattlesborough was once a sizeable hamlet, with 20 tenants in 1300 and 29 in 1379. But in 1542 there were only five taxpayers left and by 1715 the castle was the only inhabited building on the site.

The present keep dates to the late twelfth or early thirteenth century and is now incorporated into Wattlesborough Hall Farm. It is of a rather 'old fashioned' style reminiscent of earlier Norman keeps, such as Bridgnorth, though on a smaller scale, and may represent a deliberate anachronism intended to recall earlier, prestigious structures. Extending from the tower to its southeast there was once a separate hall block. Around 1712 – when the Leightons moved to Loton Park – this was demolished and replaced by the present farmhouse. Another small block, probably later than the keep itself, extends to the north-east of the tower and was accessed from it by a doorway. Constructed

134 The farm at Wattlesborough, incorporating the remains of the keep

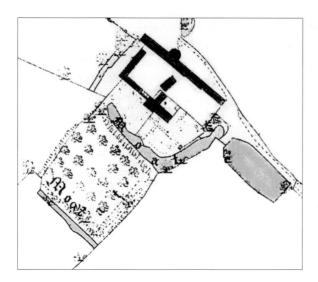

135 Wattlesborough, c.1880, showing the moats which have since been filled in

of local Alberbury breccia and red sandstone rubble, this building is shown as a gabled double-storey structure in nineteenth-century sketches.

The castle stood in a moated enclosure, the moats being doubled on the south-west front at least. Sections survived into the 1950s but have subsequently been filled in. The pond to the south-east of the building is probably an original fishpond associated with the castle.

Constructed of fine sandstone with pilaster corner buttresses, the keep offers a typically stark exterior. It is roughly 10m square with walls over 2m thick on a battered plinth and now stands to a height of approximately 12m. It was originally a two-storeyed structure raised probably in the fifteenth century by the addition of a third floor. The topmost floor had a sloping gable roof surrounded by a battlemented parapet, now gone. The lowest level or undercroft was a dark storeroom, accessed at ground level by two doors (of different dates) but only by ladder from the apartment above. Its lighting shafts are more recent. The middle floor – an attractive small chamber – had a separate entrance (now blocked) from the south-east range whilst a stairway in the east angle gave access to the upper rooms and roof. On three walls, the hall retains its original late Norman rectangular windows, now blocked, and on the north-east, a more decorated two-light window of the fourteenth century. The blocked 'Tudor' fireplace was probably inserted in the sixteenth century. The tower is now open to the sky and choked with debris, but it was roofed, floored and in use within living memory and was only gutted as its aged floor and roof timbers became unstable.

Some believe that this single keep was part of larger castle complex within the moated perimeters, with three other, smaller towers joined by curtain walls, all of which were removed in the early eighteenth century to provide material for Loton Park. There is no visible trace of any other walls or towers on the site.

Wem Castle SJ 504288

In 1086, the Saxon manor of Wem was held of Earl Roger by William Pandolf or Pantulf and later absorbed other nearby vills. William, lord of Noron near Falaise in Normandy, was one of Earl Roger's principal deputies in Shropshire. He adopted Wem as the family's main county seat and his local lands formed the powerful Barony of Wem. This descended in the Pantulf family until the thirteenth century, when it passed by marriage to the Butlers.

The original motte and bailey was probably constructed by the Pantulfs *c.*1135–50 and reconstructed in stone by Hugh Pantulf *c.*1210. It passed to the Butlers in the 1230s but appears to have fallen into decay by the 1290s.

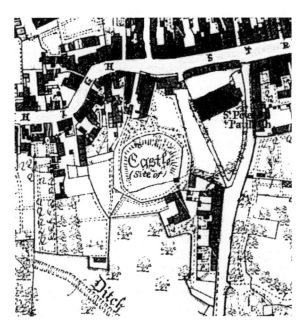

136 Wem town centre, showing the location of the castle mound

137 The low mound which is all that now remains of Wem Castle. From the churchyard

However, under the tenancy of Hugh Fitz Aer, the castle was rebuilt *c.*1310 and remained in use into the mid-fifteenth century, when it passed to the Audley family. It was dismantled *c.*1460. Evidence suggests that its military function had so far declined by then – or earlier – that house building had encroached into the castle perimeters.

Wem was unusual in that it avoided declaring for either side early in the Civil War but in September 1643 it was occupied and fortified by a Parliamentary army. They repulsed a Royalist attack led by lord Capel on 17 October, before new town defences were completed. Thereafter, Wem became the principal Parliamentary headquarters in Shropshire, defeating further Royalist attacks in April 1644 and May 1645. There is no evidence that the castle was used during the war, though the town itself was temporarily protected by an earth bank and rampart. A seventeenth-century map shows a windmill as the only structure on the motte.

The castle at Wem could easily be missed. Located in the town centre and only metres from the west door of the early medieval church of St Peter and St Paul, it is surrounded by later development and lies entirely within a private garden. The motte is very eroded after generations of robbing of its materials. Large blocks of sandstone, presumed to have been re-used from the castle, have been found in buildings around the town and there are eighteenth-

and nineteenth-century accounts of the deliberate reduction of the mound and the removal of part of its infill and masonry. Only a low, sloping fragment of the north side of the motte remains, little over 3m high and extending to about 28 x 35m. Its surrounding ditch was about 7m wide, but was filled in after 1750 and only a shallow trace remains visible to the south. There is no sign of a bailey, but it presumably lay in the area incorporating the church and graveyard.

West Felton Motte SJ 340252 ★

Feltone was recorded as 'waste' and of no value in 1086 and was held of Reginald 'the Sheriff' by a 'man at arms'. The manor later passed to the Fitz Alans and was held of them by the le Strange family.

The mound at West Felton appears to be a double motte – a large mound with a smaller one in its centre, giving a stepped effect. The circular lower motte is approximately 2.5m high, with a summit diameter of 40m, with the upper mound standing 2m high and 18m in diameter. However, it has been suggested that this stepping may not be original but the result of later garden landscaping associated with the nearby farm.

138 The tree covered 'double motte' at West Felton (centre). Note the proximity of the church (right)

The motte is surrounded by a wide ditch, which is masonry-lined and water-filled on its south-eastern side and is clearly discernible as a dry feature in the fields to the north and west. It is another Shropshire motte in close proximity to a church, standing just north-west of the Norman church of St Michael, and it has been conjectured that a bailey encompassed the area now under the church and graveyard which is on a raised platform. However, this is not certain and it is possible that the original bailey lay to the north-east, in the area of the present farm and the field beyond it, though nothing substantial remains to confirm this.

Weston-under-Redcastle Motte sj 564292 ★

Domesday Book records that Weston, formerly in the possession of Edric 'the Wild', was held of Earl Roger by Ranulf Peverel, who may have built the castle whose motte now remains. The manor returned to Crown ownership *c*.1130 and was given in 1175 to Guy le Strange and thence passed to the Audley family. In 1277, the Audleys began the construction of Red Castle (q.v.) only 600m to the north-east, so it is likely that Weston represents its predecessor and that it was abandoned around the time of Red Castle's completion *c*.1283.

139 The large castle mound at Weston-under-Redcastle

'The Mount' at Weston, 300m north of the church of St Luke, stands on a low ridge with excellent views to its west and north towards the Welsh border and over the main Whitchurch–Shrewsbury route. The steep-sided, tree-capped mound stands over 4m high, with a base circumference of 30m. It is of earth and rubble construction and there are scatterings of rubble all around the site. The summit is concave – perhaps the result of quarrying – and only 15-18m across. There are clear traces of the ditch around the mound, especially to the south, where it is approximately 7m wide at its greatest extent, though only 0.5m deep. No traces of any bailey perimeters or defences remain. The circular mound was once considered to be simply a windmill base or a feature of the landscaping of Hawkstone Park in the 1780s.

Whattal Earthwork sj 431306

On a ridge separating the lake at Crose Mere from Whattal Moss stands a feature (marked on modern maps as an 'earthwork') which has been tentatively identified as a motte. When the site was excavated in 1894 animal bones and metal fragments were discovered, but nothing is known of a castle on this site. The area is the alleged location of the vanished village of Stockett (*Stocgete*), a 'member' of the manor of Ellesmere mentioned in the twelfth century and given to Haughmond Abbey.

Whitchurch sj 543415

The town of Whitchurch, the former Roman fortress and settlement of *Mediolanum*, was held in 1086 by Count William de Warrene. Then known as *Westune*, it occurs later as both *Album Monasterium* and *Blancminster*. Little is known of the castle of Whitchurch and its site is disputed even now. Founded before 1190, there are references to it the twelfth century, in 1240 and in 1260 whilst a reference to repairs in 1384 may imply that it had been reconstructed in stone by then. The town was also defended by a ditch and earth rampart (perhaps later replaced with stone) prior to 1400.

There are two suggested sites for the castle. Its traditional location – which should presumably be given some credence – puts it south-west of the town centre, on the aptly-named 'Castle Hill', above a brook. What may have been part of the curtain wall was standing nearby in 1760, close to the mill at Mill Street, and Victorian maps show the site in that location. But although Leland referred to the castle 'lying upon a broket' (i.e. brook) nothing has been found to confirm that this area, now built over, was in fact the site of the castle. Slight traces of ditches and fragments of stone located nearby in various excavations are not deemed to be conclusive – they may be remains of the town defences, medieval buildings or even of Roman date.

Another suggested site for the castle has been Sherrymill Hill, west of the town centre. Earthworks once visible on the hill, and later used as a windmill base, could have been a motte. One reason for preferring this location is the existence of buildings in the area close to the 'traditional' site of the castle at a time (1384) when it was still known to be in repair and would not have been built over. An area called 'the Castle' in a legal case in 1586 seems to fit more closely the Sherrymill Hill site than to the other.

Although another Royalist sympathiser, Whitchurch did not play a major role in the Civil War. The town was taken by Parliament in a sudden attack in May 1643, but was not deemed strong enough even to maintain a garrison, which implies that its castle was in poor repair, if it existed at all. Thereafter,

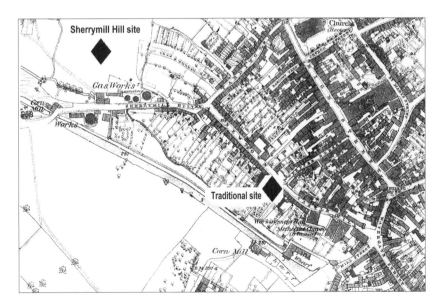

140 Whitchurch, showing possible locations of the castle

Parliamentary forces moved through and around the town but there is no evidence that the castle at Whitchurch – wherever it was – played any part in the war.

Whitsburn Hill sj 328029

On the north-west slope of Whitsburn Hill, close to the motte at Bromlow (q.v.) is a small oval enclosure which has been suggested as a ringwork. A bank with a ditch up to 9m wide, encloses an area 37m in diameter, with a possibly original entrance to the north-east. It has good views over the Rea Brook valley and may be contemporary with the mottes at Bromlow and Hope (q.v.). There is a reference to '*Wytespon*' in 1249 and to '*Whytspon*' in 1272 but nothing is known about the site. If it is a ringwork, and not a pre-medieval site or a simple farm enclosure, it is the smallest in Shropshire and presumably supported little more than a watchtower.

Whittington Castle sj 326312 ★★★

Before 1066 the wealthy manor of Whittington was a royal possession and in 1086 was held by Earl Roger himself. By the early thirteenth century it was a Marcher lordship under the Fitz Warins, a family originating from Meltz in Normandy.

Whittington Castle, 4km north-north-east of Oswestry, is an attractive site with a complex history. Standing just south of the originally medieval church of St John the Baptist, its strategic function is obscure. It is not built on a commanding height or controlling a particularly important route and its location has little to commend it from a defensive point of view, although it originally may have stood in extensive marshland. The builder of the first castle is unknown, though it has been suggested that earthworks to the south and west of the site are the remains of an Iron Age fort, later adapted as Welsh or Saxon defences. It is possible that Earl Roger himself built the first castle and there seems to have been a motte and bailey there by the late eleventh or early twelfth century. This comprised a large mound (which still remains to a height of 4.5m) with three associated baileys, perhaps of different dates – an 'inner' bailey to the east and two others to the north. The whole was defended by earth banks and wet moats. In fact, water played an important part in Whittington's defences and although parts of its moats survive near the outer gatehouse, they represent only a fraction of the original water defences which surrounded the site.

After the confiscation of Robert of Bellême's estates in 1102 the manor was given by Henry I to William Peverel of Dover. He may have begun or extended the castle at Whittington, though the first surviving reference occurs in 1138, when it was held against King Stephen by Peverel's nephew. In 1164, the manor passed to the de Vere family (related by marriage to the de Says of Clun) and received a grant for repair under Henry II in 1173. In 1204, King John gave Whittington to the Fitz Warins, relatives of the Peverel family, who held it for the next 200 years.

It is generally accepted that, whatever else was on the site, the first significant stone castle was built *c.*1215-35 by Fulke Fitz Warine (died *c.*1256). He may have built the rectangular stone keep, 15 x 11m, whose footings survive on a large raised platform in the middle of the old inner bailey; this could

141 Aerial view of the castle remains and earthworks at Whittington. *CPAT-92-MC02-07*

142 The twin
D-shaped towers
forming the gate
defences to the outer
bailey at Whittington

date to as early as *c.*1215 when he was in rebellion against King John. After
fleeing to France, Fulke was later restored to favour and bought back the site
of Whittington. Under Henry III, he received licence in 1221 to fortify the
castle, but only so much as was needed to defend it against the Welsh; the
stone curtain wall and towers of the inner bailey may be the product of this
phase. The raised rectangular platform of the stone keep was surrounded by
a limestone curtain wall, over 2m thick and 7m high, with a wall-walk and
five round towers, each about 11m in diameter, at its angles. Extensive ruins
of these walls and towers still remain, although most of their dressed facing
stone has gone. Two of the towers were paired at the north-east angle of the
walls to form an inner gateway. Much of the eastern tower of this pair, of fine
limestone construction, still stands and gives an impression of the formidable appearance of the original defences. The remains of buildings within the
walled compound were found during excavation and include a hall some 15
x 7m along the east wall, an oven and a well. Interestingly, but not uniquely,
the old motte was not included within the newly-enclosed bailey but left isolated to its west. Whittington may have been captured in 1223 by Llewellyn

ap Iorwerth, which would suggest that building work was not completed by then and layers of charcoal found in the keep may imply that it was destroyed by fire around that date.

The extensive northern baileys were never completely defended by stone walls. However, a south-east section of the north-east ward was enclosed in the mid-thirteenth century with fairly weak stone walls and towers to protect subsidiary (probably timber) buildings like stables and barns. The most distinctive feature of this bailey is the pair of D-shaped towers standing over the moat to the east, which formed the outer gateway of the castle. Its towers protected the entrance, now approached across the moat by a restored bridge of limestone rubble. The battlements and roofs on the towers are nineteenth-century or later restorations, as are other features like the upper windows. The block survived because it remained in fairly continuous occupation as a house and in the late seventeenth century a cottage (now much altered) was constructed behind it.

Granted to the Welsh prince Llewellyn ap Gruffydd (along with other border castles and lands) in 1265, Whittington was restored to the Fitz Warins in 1282 following the defeat of the Welsh by Edward I. The castle again saw action against the Welsh during the rebellion of Owain Glyndwr in 1405, but was not captured.

143 One of the impressive round towers of the inner bailey gateway at Whittington

Around 1415, Whittington passed by marriage to Sir William Bouchier, afterwards Earl of Bath, and was later granted by Henry VI to the Earl of Stafford. From then on, the castle slowly fell into ruin. By the 1540s, when Leland saw little worthy of report, it was empty and dilapidated and thereafter began to be robbed of its stone and materials. Despite a reference to Royalist forces taking 'the passage of water near to Whittington' to attack Oswestry in June 1644, it is not clear that the castle played any part in the Civil War and its later history is obscure.

Around 1760 the south-east tower fell into the moat – apparently after a severe frost – and one of the northern towers and part of the west wall were demolished shortly afterwards to provide material for the Whittington–Halston road; in 1809 and as late as 1898 stone was also removed to repair the outer gatehouse. The grounds seem to have been laid out as a decorative rectory garden in the late eighteenth century and as a public park in the late nineteenth century. Nowadays, the site is owned by the local community and cared for by the Whittington Castle Preservation Trust, which has contributed enormously to the preservation and interpretation of the site.

Wilcott Motte sj 379185 ★

Wilcott was part of the manor of Ness, which descended in the le Strange family. The motte lies in an angle of the modern crossroads, at the northern end of a natural bank east of Wilcott village and 140m south-east of Wilcott Hall. The well-defined circular motte has a base diameter of 42m and stands on the tip of a spur, overlooking a stream to its west and using the natural strength of the site to good effect. To the north-west, the slope of the motte merges into the natural fall of the spur; here, its summit stands over 9m above the marshy ground which offered some defence in that direction so that no ditch was necessary. However, to the south of the site, where the slope of the spur rises away from the motte, the mound is only 4m high and on this side is defended by a curved ditch 4m wide and now only 0.2m deep, cut across the spur. The northern part of the site overlooks the road and the defences to the east may have been damaged by road construction along that side.

The summit of the tree-covered motte has a diameter of approximately 26m, with its interior dug away to form a distinct depression some 21m across. This has led to the site being regarded as a ringwork, with an earth rampart. However, the depression may represent the robbed-out base of a

144 Part of the earthwork at Wilcott

circular stone tower which originally stood on the summit. The south-western quarter of the bank around the edge of the depression has been cut through, creating an entrance 4m wide, though it may not be original. There are no traces of a bailey associated with the site.

Wilderley Motte and Bailey SJ 433016 ★

Wilderley was one of three manors held of Earl Roger by Hugh 'son of Thorgils'. All reverted to the Crown after the rebellion of Robert de Bellême in 1102 and ultimately became part of the Honour of Montgomery, given by Henry I to Baldwin de Boulers. In the thirteenth century Wilderley was granted to Haughmond Abbey.

The motte and bailey stands 150m south-west of Wilderley Hall Farm. The steep-sided motte rises to 6m, with a flat summit 16m in diameter. Although well-defined, it is now overgrown by bushes and trees. Its position on the slopes of a spur affords fine views in all directions, especially to the east and north (towards Castle Pulverbatch (q.v.)). The surrounding ditch is visible on all but the south-eastern side and extends to 4-6m wide and up to 1.5m deep. It is marshy in wet weather. A considerable amount of rubble is strewn around the site.

There are two baileys – or one large enclosure divided into two sections by a low bank – lying to the east of the mound, on the downhill slope towards the

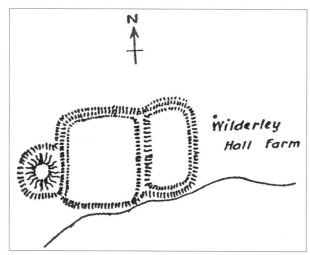

Above: 145 The motte at Wilderley, now entirely shrouded in trees, from the inner bailey

Left: 146 The motte and bailey site at Wilderley. *VCH/1*

farm. The overall size is approximately 100 x 80m. The platform of the 'inner' bailey – nearest the motte – and traces of its surrounding ditch are visible on the southern side of the site, where there are signs of a possible entrance to the enclosure. There are also traces of perimeter banks on the north side of the bailey.

Willaston Motte SJ 597359

Willaston was one of the 'members' of the manor of Prees and has no separate reference in Domesday Book. All that survives of the castle is a low, tree-covered circular mound, 2m high and 15m across its summit, surrounded by a

147 The low castle mound at Willaston, surrounded by its deep ditch. No trace of a bailey exists

well-defined ditch up to 1m deep and 4m wide, with a slight outer bank. The location of its bailey has not been traced.

The motte stands just north of Willaston Farm and only 60m south-west of a moated mansion site which may represent the later residence of the owners of Willaston.

Wilmington Motte SJ 433017 ★

Despite its Saxon origins, *Wilmitun* has no entry in Domesday Book, though it may have been one of the extensive holdings attached to Montgomery Castle under Earl Roger.

'The Mount' is an imposing motte about 150m north-east of Wilmington Farm. Standing on an artificially scarped and shaped ridge to the south of the Rea Brook, it overlooks Marton Pool and the valley route between Montgomery and Shrewsbury (*colour plate 30*). The castles at Wilmington and Marton (q.v.) would have controlled both sides of the valley. The largely circular mound is approximately 4.5m high with a summit diameter of 8m and a base of 30-32m. Stone fragments on the summit and around the site have been interpreted as the remains of a former gazebo but may be actual remnants of earlier structures on the mound. At the time of writing, the motte is being badly damaged by badgers.

A pear-shaped bailey, constricted by the natural lie of the land on the top of the ridge, surrounds the mound, its largest area fanning out to the north of the motte. Little trace remains of defensive ditches and banks apart from a low scarp, which is most pronounced to the north of the site.

Winsbury Motte SO 246984

Winsbury, 1.5km west of Chirbury, was a dependency of the Honour of Montgomery and descended into the hands of the de Winsbury family. The village lies 1.2km east of Offa's Dyke, with the motte at East Dudston (q.v.) only 1km to its south. A motte, approx 25m in diameter and up to 5m high stood north of the farm in Winsbury and was surrounded by a ditch 3-4m deep. Damaged by farm building work in the 1870s, the rest was removed in 1961. Emergency excavations found thirteenth-century pottery, which ties in with its tenure by the de Winsburys, its tenants throughout the thirteenth century. The bailey may have stood to the south and south-west, the location of the present farm.

Wollaston Motte SJ 328123 ★

In 1086, Wollaston was held of Earl Roger by Roger Fitz Corbet of the Corbets of Caus and he or his family presumably built the motte and bailey there. It stands on high ground overlooking the main Shrewsbury–Welshpool route. Modern buildings encroach upon the site to its south and east, but

148 The impressive castle mound at Wollaston, with the nearby church of St John

'The Mount' remains an impressive steep-sided motte, rising some 8-9m from ground level. It is surrounded on all sides except the east by a well-defined ditch at least 1m deep. The D-shaped bailey is defined by a faint bank and shallow ditch to the north and north-west but was partially destroyed by the construction of the late eighteenth-century church of St John to the east. This stands on the site of an early medieval chapel which may have been associated with the castle.

About 500m to the south-west, in fields between the present A458 and the railway line (map ref. SJ 324120), are the ploughed-away traces of a ringwork, once known as 'Caesar's Camp' or 'The Moat'. It now barely rises above the surrounding land and has only the slightest traces of an earth rampart and ditch. Nothing is known of its history but it may have been intended to complement the castle at Wollaston, controlling the valley route at this point.

Woolstaston Motte SO 450985

By 1086, the manor of Woolstaston was one of 15 held of Earl Roger by Robert Fitz Corbet. His family were given large holdings of territory as part of the policy of creating a barrier along the Welsh border. Excavations in 1965 produced pottery of the twelfth and thirteenth centuries but the site appears to have been abandoned by the fourteenth century. The manor later passed into the hands of the Botterell family.

The motte stands in a strong defensive position on 'Castle Bank', a hill to the west of the village, 150m west of the church. Smethcott motte (q.v.) stands

149 The site of the bailey on the ridge at Woolstaston

1km to the north, on the opposite side of the valley known as Betchcott
Hollow. The mound and its triangular bailey lies along the top of a steep-
sided hill which has been additionally shaped, giving extensive views to the
north, west and east. The motte is about 3m high and 9m across its summit, with a base diameter of 18m, and lies at the west end of the bailey. Its
surrounding ditch is no longer visible, though excavations in 1965 revealed
its presence as a buried feature. The southern side of the bailey falls steeply to
the present main road whose course may follow the original bailey ditch on
that side. The north side of the bailey, facing a slighter slope, has an additional
earth rampart, though no trace of a ditch is visible on that side.

The site has been encroached upon in recent times by a water reservoir built
into the north end of the bailey and a large house which cuts into the west face
of the motte and whose garden impinges upon the south-west side of the site.

Worsley Earthworks SO 461959

On Castle Hill, an isolated outlier of the Long Mynd, stand the earthwork
ramparts and ditches of Worsley castle. From its location 70m above a stream
at All Stretton, it commands the north-south route towards Church Stretton.
It makes good use of the natural strength of the location, the hill having
been artificially shaped to the north, east and west whilst the southern side

150 Part of the earthwork defences at Worsley Bank

is defended by the steep fall of the hillside. The roughly rectangular and level platform extends to approximately 20 x 22m, defended by two concentric banks. There are traces of a ditch and bank on the west' and a possible entrance to the south-east. A flat space to the east, possibly defined by hedge banks at right angles to each other, may be the location of the bailey. It has been suggested that the site adapts an existing Iron Age fort and that it was the predecessor to the castle at Brockhurst (q.v.)

Wotherton Motte sj 283007 ★

Wotherton manor was held at the time of Domesday from Earl Roger by Alward, son of Almund and later became part of the Honour of Montgomery.

The motte stands in the grounds of Wotherton Farm on a spur with commanding views along the valleys of the Aylesford and Camlad, though it is overlooked by high ground to its south. The mound stands to a height of approximately 3m with a flat summit 9 x 10m across. A surrounding ditch is visible on all but the north-west side, where the fall of land into the valley provides a strong defensive slope. No trace of a bailey remains but it is likely that it lay to the south, where the farm now stands.

Wroxeter sj 562081

The village standing amongst the remains of the Roman town at Wroxeter was held in 1086 by Rainald (Reginald), Sheriff of Shropshire, and later formed part of the demesne lands of the Fitz Alans of Oswestry. A castle or manor house built by Reginald or the Fitz Alans is reputed to have stood in the village. However, excavations on its presumed site near a ford on the Severn south-west of the Saxon church revealed nothing conclusive; masonry recovered there could not be positively identified as Roman or medieval.

Yockleton Motte sj 396103 ★

At the time of Domesday, Yockleton was one of many manors held from Earl Roger by Roger Fitz Corbet.

151 The small motte at Wotherton, overlooking the Aylesford and Camlad rivers (to the right)

152 The tree-covered motte at Yockleton from the north

The motte, now an overgrown oval mound approximately 4m high, was built on a well-chosen site with clear views in all directions. It stood on the eastern end of a ridge overlooking the Yockleton Brook and commanded its medieval crossing and the Shrewsbury road beyond. The base of the mound is approximately 33 x 44m, rising to a flat summit of 24 x 14m, and is steepest on its northern face. Around the site there is much evidence of rubble especially in the field to the north and in the fabric of the mound itself. The ditch is traceable on all but the south side, though generally very shallow, and is most pronounced on the weaker western side of the site, from where, presumably, any approach to the castle must have been made. Here, it is still up to 2m deep and 6m wide. There are no visible traces of a bailey, which may have lain to the north in what is now ploughed land.

BIBLIOGRAPHY

Acton, Mrs. S., *The Garrisons of Shropshire*, Leake and Evans, Shrewsbury, 1867

Acton, Mrs. S., *The Castles and Old Mansions of Shropshire, 1142-1660*, Leake and Evans, Shrewsbury, 1868

Alcock, L. and King, D.J.C., 'Ringworks of England and Wales', *Chateau Gaillard*, 1969, Vol. 3, pp. 90-127

Beaumont, H., *Shrewsbury Castle : a Brief History*, Wildings, Shrewsbury, 1977

Bracher, T. and Emmett, R., *Shropshire in the Civil War*, Shropshire Books, Shrewsbury 2000

Camden, W., *Britannia*, Eliot, London, 1586; facsimile ed., Olms, Hildesheim, 1970

Cathcart King, D.J., *Castellarium Anglicanum*, Kraus International, New York, 1983

Chitty, L., 'Subsidiary Castle Sites West of Shrewsbury', *Transactions of the Shropshire Archaeological Society*, 1949; Vol. 53; pp. 83-90

Clwyd and Powys Archaeological Trust, Welshpool: aerial photographs

Colvin, H.M. (ed.), *History of the King's Works*, HMSO, London, 6 vols, 1963-82

Eyton, R.W., *The Antiquities of Shropshire*, 12 vols, London, 1853-60

Farrow, W.J., *The Civil War in Shropshire*, Wilding, Shrewsbury, 1926

Foxall, H.D.G. (comp.), *A Gazetteer of Streets, Roads and Place names in Shropshire*, Salop County Council, Shrewsbury, 1967

Gravett, C., *Norman Stone Castles, The British Isles 1066-1216*, Osprey Books, 2003

Hampton, C., *Ludlow Castle*, Guion and King, Sheffield, 1977

Higham, R. and Barker, P., *Timber Castles*, University of Exeter Press, Exeter, 2004

Hogg, A.H.A. and King, D.J.C., 'Early castles in Wales and the Marches: a preliminary list', *Archaeologia Cambrensis*, Vol. 112, 1963

Hogg, A.H.A. and King, D.J.C, 'Masonry Castles in Wales and The Marches: A list', *Archaeologia Cambrensis*, 1967; Vol. 116; pp 71-132

Jackson, M., *Castles of Shropshire*, Shropshire Libraries, Shrewsbury, 1988

King, D.J.C., *Castellarium Anglicanum*, Kraus International Publications, Millwood, New York, 1983

Leach, F., *Select views of the Antiquities of Shropshire*, Eddowes, Shrewsbury, 1891

Leonard, J., *The Churches of Shropshire and their Treasures*, Logaston Press, Almeley, 2004

Mason, Dr. J.F.A., *Stokesay Castle*, English Life Publications, 1974

Meisel, J., *Barons of the Welsh Frontier 1066-1272*, University of Nebraska Press, Nebraska, 1980

Millward, R. and Robinson, A., *The Welsh Borders*, Eyre Methuen, London, 1978

Mitchell, R., *A Short History of the Old Hall and Manor of Cressage*, Robin Mitchell, Shrewsbury, 2003

Morris, J.A. and Beaumont, H., *Shrewsbury Castle*, Wildings, Shrewsbury, 1965.

Morris, J. (ed.), *The Domesday Book (Shropshire)*, Phillimore, Chichester, 1986.

O'Neil, B.H.StJ., *Castles: an introduction to the Castles of England and Wales*, HMSO, 1974

Ordnance Survey: *Landranger* series (1:50,0000): sheets 117, 118, 126, 127, 136, 137, 138

Ordnance Survey: 1880s editions, mainly 1:25,000

Pearson, Wm., *Select Views of the Antiquities of Shropshire*, London, 1807

Pevsner, N., *The Buildings of England (Shropshire)*, Penguin, Harmondsworth, 1958 and 1974

Ralegh Radford, C.A., *Acton Burnell Castle*, HMSO, 1977

Renn, D., *Norman Castles in Britain*, J. Baker/Humanities Press, London, 1973

Rowley, T., *The Welsh Border: Archaeology, History and Landscape*, Tempus, Stroud, 2001 edition

Rowley, T., *Norman England,* Batsford, London, 1997

Salter, M., *The Castles and Moated Mansions of Shropshire*, Folly Publications, Malvern, 1988 and 2001

Salter, M., *Midland Castles*, Quercus, Birmingham, 1993

Shropshire Archaeological Society, *Transactions*, various dates

Shropshire Sites and Monument Record Cards, various dates

Timmins, H.T., *Nooks and Corners of Shropshire*, Stock, London 1899 and reprint Lapridge Publications, Hereford, 1993

Toulmin-Smith, L., *Leland's Itinerary in England and Wales*, South Illinois University Press, 1980

Victoria County History, Shropshire, Vol. 1, 1908

Watson, M., *Shropshire: An Archaeological Guide*, Shropshire Books, Shrewsbury, 2002

Watson, M. and Musson, C., *Shropshire from the Air: Man and the Landscape*, Shropshire Books, Shrewsbury, 1993